UNFILTERED

A HANDBOOK ON HOW TO
COMBAT MISINFORMATION

UNFILTERED

A HANDBOOK ON HOW TO
COMBAT MISINFORMATION

SUDIKSHA KOCHI

NEW DEGREE PRESS
COPYRIGHT © 2022 SUDIKSHA KOCHI
All rights reserved.

UNFILTERED
A Handbook on How to Combat Misinformation
ISBN   979-8-88504-142-3 Paperback
           979-8-88504-775-3 Kindle Ebook
           979-8-88504-254-3 Ebook

To all high schoolers, college students, early-career journalists, and professionals wanting to help combat misinformation.

And, to all the little girls out there who want to be journalists or authors who can read this book and know they can get there one day.

TABLE OF CONTENTS

INTRODUCTION		9
PART 1		**13**
CHAPTER 1	WHAT IS FAKE NEWS? AND WHY DO PEOPLE KEEP SAYING IT?	15
CHAPTER 2	MY FIRST ENCOUNTER RIGHTING A WRONG: "HE'S DEAD!"	27
CHAPTER 3	SOCIAL MEDIA INS AND OUTS	39
CHAPTER 4	VIDEO GAMES AND CONSPIRACY THEORIES: HOW ARE THEY RELATED?	53
CHAPTER 5	UNCOVERING THE PSYCHOLOGY OF MISINFORMATION	65
PART 2		**77**
CHAPTER 6	STORIES OF THOSE WHO FELL INTO THE RABBIT HOLE AND ACTIVIST EFFORTS TAKEN TO COMBAT FALSEHOODS	79
CHAPTER 7	WHAT THESE STORIES TAUGHT ME AND WHAT YOU CAN LEARN	89
CHAPTER 8	JOURNALISTS' INSIGHT INTO BUILDING TRUST	101
CHAPTER 9	MY TAKE ON HOW TO COMBAT MISINFORMATION	113
ACKNOWLEDGMENTS		123
APPENDIX		127

INTRODUCTION

PERFECTION IS ALMOST IMPOSSIBLE TO ATTAIN

My journey in combating misinformation has not been easy. And that includes writing this book. I've written this book three times. Yes, *three times*. Let me tell you, this task was not easy, but I've come to acknowledge misinformation is not an easy concept to understand either. So why was I so invested in doing this project? Here is a little story for you.

A year ago, I was sitting at my desk with my laptop and a thought going through my head: What if I wrote a book?

My dream had always been to be a published author, but more importantly, I wanted to produce something that would impact people in a positive way, so I started the long and hard process of figuring out what I wanted my book to be about.

I initially wanted to write about the changing media landscape and how more people were getting their news through social media. But, as I immersed myself in my research, I quickly realized there was more to Instagram, Facebook, Twitter, and other platforms than one might think. Misinformation was a term I had come across in my research, and as an early-career reporter, I couldn't help but dig into this mystery a bit more.

That's when my eyes opened. I looked at the conspiracy theories fact-checkers had written about and debunked. I looked at what people were saying on my social media feed about the outcome of the presidential election and the coronavirus pandemic.

For four months, I went back and forth between the books I was reading and the research I was finding online until January 6, 2021, when hundreds of people—who believed the presidential election was a fraud—stormed Capitol Hill. That is when I realized the impact of misinformation, how dangerous it can be, and why we shouldn't fall into its trap.

From doing tons of research to conducting interviews to including methods I would use based on my experiences interning at three newsrooms and taking online journalism courses, I have compiled chapters of strategies to help you avoid, spot, and fight misinformation. But the goal with this book was to do more than just that.

I wanted people to understand *why* misinformation spreads and what drives people to believe in falsehoods, which is where I think the underlying root of the problem is. I've always been so fascinated in the psychology behind misinformation and conspiracies, a topic I explore in this book.

If you are just starting your journey in debunking falsehoods, this book will be both effective and efficient in helping you get to where you need to be. It features:

- Interviews from researchers, video-game experts, and psychiatrists on the psychology behind misinformation.

- An in-depth look at social media algorithms and how they work in real-time.
- A story from a victim of QAnon, a conspiracy theory, and activist ways to combat misinformation.
- Voices from journalists on building trust with communities.
- My take on misinformation, including tactics I use on social media.

This book should be a tool you can use to positively impact your life. Once you are done reading it, I recommend sharing your insights with your friends, family members, and acquaintances, so they can also start their journey if they haven't already. It is by no means perfect, and research in this field is still going on. But what I am sharing with you is what people, including me, have discovered on our journeys.

And one more thing.

To all of you reading this book, whether it be in two months or even a year from now, thank you. Thank you for being a part of the journey. Thank you for being a part of my dream. Thank you for taking time out of your day to immerse yourself in the pages I have put all my energy, time, and effort into. Thank you.

PART ONE

PART ONE

CHAPTER ONE
WHAT IS FAKE NEWS? AND WHY DO PEOPLE KEEP SAYING IT?

I am a very curious person, and my curiosity is naturally what drove me to search up the words "what is fake news?" on my laptop one faithful afternoon in 2020. Pundits, politicians, and press critics had thrown around the phrase for as long as I could remember, and a certain negative stigma to it frustrated and flabbergasted me every time I heard it.

Whether it was a friend, a family member, or a stranger, the slightest whisper or echo of the phrase felt like a pin dropping on my foot.

"Oh, that's wrong. That's *fake news.*"

"Omg, *fake news* at its finest."

"*Fake news! Fake news! Fake news!*"

As an early-career journalist, I knew the harmful implications fake news carried. I've worked at three different newsrooms, so I've seen firsthand the extensive research, interviewing, and writing that goes into producing an article for the public to read. But, when someone says fake news, the term often transforms into an instrument used to discredit the work of reporters.

How do I know this? Because right after they say this phrase, I typically hear these words too: *"It's all the media's fault! Don't trust journalists!"* Where is this coming from? And have we always used the phrase like this? The answers to these questions are kind of muddled.

First, it is important to take a step back and understand how the changing definition of fake news has impacted journalism, particularly regarding the relationship between readers and reporters.

We can interpret fake news in many ways today. People can use fake news to refer to inaccurate or misleading information. People can use it to refer to facts they don't like hearing. We've heard the phrase so much it has become second nature for us to say it when we hear information that sounds surreal or out of the blue.

All these instances are exactly what has made the definition of fake news arbitrary—because no one can agree on what it truly means.

Researchers and academics have applied the term in their studies, and it has referred to news that contained falsehoods. Hunt Allcott, assistant professor of economics at New York University, and Matthew Gentzkow, professor of economics at Stanford University, published a study on "Social Media and Fake News in the 2016 election" in the *Journal of Economic Perspectives.* They define fake news well: "news articles that are intentionally and verifiably false and could mislead readers" (Allcott and Gentzkow, 2017).

The research study places a focus on fabricated news articles and satirical articles misinterpreted as factual news. Let's get a closer look at these two categories before we move further into this phenomenon so you can get a small taste of how researchers have looked at "fake news."

A small disclaimer: I'll be defining these terms from what *I've* occasionally found on social media and the internet, so it doesn't pertain to any particular study. But the examples I am about to introduce have been explored by researchers before.

In the world of falsehoods, fabricated is a common term used by many people. According to Merriam-Webster, the literal definition is "to make up for the purpose of deception." Fabricated news articles are created and circulated online with the *intent to mislead people.*

I've seen several types of fabricated news articles on social media. The most common one I've encountered online stems from websites that impersonate mainstream media. The way they do this is simple: an imitation of URLs and logos. That website publishes articles that contain hoaxes, conspiracy theories, and falsehoods.

You might be thinking, *how can a person imitate a URL?* There are some tricks to it.

At first glance, any social media user who comes across an article shared with the link ABCnews.com.co on their Facebook feed might be quick to believe it is the actual *ABC News* sharing the information, especially since the copyrighted name is in the link. But a quick search on google for the actual *ABC News* link, which goes by abcnews.go.com, will prove otherwise.

If you are curious about the ABCnews.com.co link, yes, that was a real website, and I have come across it. Paul Horner, who was well known for performing this type of fraud, was responsible for it, according to a 2017 article fact-check reporter Daniel Funke published for the Poynter Institute titled "Weeks after his death, most of Paul Horner's fake news sites are down. So what's left?" (Funke, 2017).

One article shared through the link claimed former President Barack Obama signed an executive order to ban the pledge of allegiance in schools across the country. I remember this clearly because a friend of mine had a discussion with a teacher about it when I was in high school. At the time, I knew nothing about the article, but fact-check reporter Caroline Wallace confirmed the article was satirical and came from ABCnews.com.co in a 2016 article titled "Obama did not ban the pledge" on factcheck.org (Wallace, 2016).

When encountering links like these, seeing if the website has a note attached anywhere with a name is also helpful, whether it be in the about section or right underneath an article. If a name is posted, do a quick google search on who that person is. Chances are, you will most likely find out where the information is coming from.

A fabricated news article can also use sensationalized headlines that make it look like the information is accurate even though it is not. The headline gives an authoritative appeal to the article. A good example of this is *Real Raw News*, a website that regularly publishes misinformation. One of the headlines used in an article said, "Military arrests SCJ Sonia Sotomayor." A quick thirty-second google search confirms this never happened.

Satire, on the other hand, is when someone makes a humorous piece about an issue. The problem with satire is when a person has trouble understanding the humor behind it and takes the piece seriously. Common satire sites include the *Babylon Bee* and the *Onion*. We'll get more into this category in the next chapter.

Fake news' varies in the context of research it is used in. For instance, Allcott and Gentzkow define the boundary of what fake news is and isn't in their study by stating "unintentional reporting mistakes" and conspiracies don't count as fake news. But it is understood, at least by most outside experts, fake news consists of articles that intentionally contain falsehoods.

Now, let's flip the coin to the other widely known usage of fake news people have adopted, tied to the principle of confirmation bias: a person believes in information they encounter if it aligns with their already established beliefs.

There's a lot to unpack here with this one, but it might be easier to understand with a real-world example. During his presidency, former president Donald Trump was known for repeatedly saying fake news whenever the media published factual news he didn't like. The repetitive use of the phrase left the impression no one should trust journalists, and it influenced the public the more it was repeated.

The events of January 6, 2021 really tested the boundaries of how powerful the phrase can be when thrown around. On that day, thousands stormed Capitol Hill spreading the belief the 2020 presidential election was a fraud. The culmination of events that led to the insurrection was in part due to the lack of trust the people held with the media, instigated by the phrase "fake news" that deemed the media an enemy.

The usage of fake news in this manner is problematic, and while confirmation bias plays a role, so does access to quality journalism. Not everyone has a laptop they can use daily to log on to websites like *The Washington Post, The New York Times,* and so forth to get caught up on the latest happenings, and that's how they are more likely to be exposed to misleading content.

So which side of the debate am I on? Should we keep saying fake news or not? Personally, I think not. Bill Adair, PolitiFact founder and Knight professor of the practice of journalism and public policy, explored this phenomenon with me further in an interview.

"Fake news is a phrase that has become essentially meaningless because it means different things to everyone," Adair said.

He added misinformation and disinformation are terms that should refer to inaccurate or misleading content. Fact-checking organizations, such as PolitiFact, First Draft, and Full Fact, use these terms.

"We have a serious problem in this country believing falsehoods about the coronavirus and the outcome of the 2020 presidential election. And that is scary," Adair said. "People have so much access to information, yet they keep on believing in the wrong things. It has worried me we've gotten into this situation."

MISINFORMATION VS. DISINFORMATION

The distinctions between misinformation and disinformation are clear. A little disclaimer, though: every expert has their own way of thinking about and defining these two terms. Let's start with what experts are saying about the latter.

I interviewed Jon Roozenbeek, a British Academy postdoctoral fellow at Cambridge University. He said what most people understand by disinformation is a deliberate and organized campaign to spread and popularize information that is not primarily intended to inform people.

He added the goal of these campaigns is to sow divisions between groups in society, and that can take place through the spread of false information, which reduces trust in the government and other institutions.

"We call it disinformation if these kinds of tactics are used by foreign entities, government entities, and political entities with a particular political or geopolitical goal in mind," Roozenbeek said.

A good example of this is with Russian disinformation campaigns. Graphika, a company that uses artificial intelligence to explore social media campaigns, published a report in 2020 analyzing close to 2,500 pieces of content published by Secondary Infektion, a Russian campaign, posted over a six-year period (Graphika, 2020). Some of the content focused on disinformation concerning the 2016 presidential election in the US.

What I found most fascinating about the study was, in addition to forged documents, the people behind Secondary Infektion commonly concealed their identities. They would use multiple accounts that would have one post each as opposed to a single account with multiple posts, according to Graphika. Foreign actors are not the only ones to spread disinformation though, Roozenbeek said.

"The problem is all of these tactics and strategies that are used by the Russians, you can easily use them yourself if you want to," Roozenbeek said. "They're not specifically beholden to foreign entities for any reason, right? And so that's where the definition gets a bit muddy."

Intent, as Roozenbeek describes, can refer to an organized campaign aimed at destabilizing particular countries or governments or other entities. But obviously, people who aren't part of these supposed campaigns still spread disinformation in some circumstances. Intent, in this case, still exists.

I interviewed Emily Vraga, professor of journalism at the University of Minnesota, who told me disinformation is when knowingly false information is deliberately spread to advance some kind of political, strategic, social, or financial goal. These goals don't necessarily have to be tied to a larger campaign.

A good example of this would be if someone is claiming the COVID-19 vaccine causes infertility. According to the Centers for Disease Control and Prevention (CDC), it does not. However, an outside party or singular person could pay someone, for that matter, to spread this information, knowing it is false, with the goal of having people not get the vaccine.

Scams are also an effective method of disinformation. For instance, I came across a link to a website on Facebook that claimed the Pfizer-BioNTech and Moderna COVID-19 vaccines were ineffective. It also had a picture and name of a vaccine that was being marketed as the "official cure" for COVID-19. From the marketing, it was clear the website was set up for some sort of financial gain, but anyone could fall for its trap.

A 2021 study titled the "Disinformation Dozen" published by the Center for Countering Digital Hate found 65 percent of the antivaccine content shared or posted to Facebook and Twitter close to 812,000 times between February 1 and March 16, 2021 came from twelve antivaxxers (Center for Countering Digital Hate, 2021).

"They are creating it often with a financial purpose, sometimes with a political purpose," Vraga said.

But if my mom shared an antivaccine post from Robert F. Kennedy Jr.'s social media account without a strategic purpose in mind, would that still be disinformation? No, which brings us to our next topic of concern: misinformation.

Misinformation is when some level of falsehood is spread online. However, Roozenbeek said having a definition that focuses just on falsehood is incomplete because information could also be taken out of context and be labeled as misinformation.

For instance, Roozenbeek encountered a headline of an article that read "a healthy doctor died two weeks after receiving a COVID vaccine."

"The problem is the implication of this headline is this doctor died because he got vaccinated, which isn't true, or at least there's no evidence for that," Roozenbeek said.

If someone took a screenshot of that same article and shared it on Facebook, you might come across the image and think that's exactly what happened, when it is quite the contrary. If context is missing, that is a sign you could be misled about a situation.

"What I tend to do, and what we tend to do in our lab, is focus on content you can recognize as misleading or manipulative," Roozenbeek said. "Usually when you read a headline on social media, you can detect whether someone is using a particular strategy to increase the number of clicks or mislead people while leaving out important context (from the actual article)."

If it meets one of those criteria, Roozenbeek said it might fall on the misinformation spectrum. Intent is really where the difference between misinformation and disinformation comes into play. Disinformation is essentially a subcategory of misinformation, but when it comes to misinformation, you can't assume intent.

"Anything that is disinformation is misinformation. Disinformation just adds a layer on top of it that says this is not just false, it's knowingly false, and it's done for some strategic purpose," Vraga said.

The question of intent and knowingness is hard to discern, Vraga said. The way I like to think about it is this: if I share a falsehood on social media I don't know is false, or I believe in the falsehood myself, then that would count as misinformation. The definition can get confusing if I spread something that was initially shared as disinformation. Intent, in this case, would be hard to assume, because an outside person wouldn't know whether I did it to advance a goal.

Vraga put it in a neat way: disinformation is about intent or using inaccurate information to advance a goal. Misinformation, on the other hand, is about the veracity of the information itself, and whether it's accurate. That can be complicated too, she adds.

"Deciding whether or not something is misinformation should be dependent on the amount of data you have, and expert consensus to help us evaluate whether that data is relevant, whether it's solid, whether it's appropriate ... based on the best available evidence from relevant experts at any given point in time," Vraga said.

PREBUNKING VS. DEBUNKING MISINFORMATION

Now we know a bit about what misinformation is, we still have a series of questions awaiting us: How does someone combat misinformation? And who does the work here? Here are two terms to know in light of these questions: prebunking and debunking.

During my spring semester of college, I worked at PolitiFact, an independent fact-checking organization operated by the Poynter Institute in St. Petersburg, Florida. In a United Facts of America festival hosted by PolitiFact in 2021, Poynter Institute President Neil Brown exposed a shocking revelation over a prerecorded zoom session later uploaded to YouTube: PolitiFact was founded on a lie (PolitiFact, 2021).

"The legend is it really started at the 2004 Republican National Convention when a Democrat was giving a speech we were not fact-checking," Adair said in the session. "I was then working for the *St. Petersburg Times,* and we were all in New York and Zell Miller [Democratic politician] was giving this speech that was filled with a lot of half-truths."

That's when the idea for PolitiFact started. Angie Holan, Matt Waite, Brown, and Adair launched the infamous Truth-O-Meter to rate politicians' and social media claims. This meter's ratings range from true, mostly true, half true, mostly false, false, to *pants on fire.*

What PolitiFact does is *debunking,* which means investigating and fact-checking information typically after it has reached some level of virality. The information is rated depending on where it fits the Truth-O-Meter. A little disclaimer: *pants on fire* is probably my favorite rating.

The second fact check I've ever written in my entire journalism career was a *pants on fire* fact check on March 17, 2021. It was about a viral screenshot of a tweet circulating on Facebook that read "Oprah was gagged, okay?" The tweet included three pictures of Winfrey from her blockbuster interview with Meghan Markle on March 7, 2021.

Anyone who came across the post would believe Markle was the one behind the tweet since the handle of the account was @MeghanMarkleHRH. But this handle comes from a parody account, and Markle doesn't have a Twitter account to begin with. I debunked the claim.

Debunking is directly responsive to a falsehood that has become viral. Someone makes a claim and fact-check reporters determine whether that claim is true using facts, expert comment, and scientific research. Prebunking is designed to happen before the misinformation starts spreading.

"To be successful, we want to do two things. Ideally, we want to warn people misinformation is likely," Vraga said. "And two, we want to give them strategies to recognize it and to resist its influence."

According to Vraga, there are two main types of prebunking: fact-based and rhetorical. Fact-based prebunking occurs when experts can outline the facts of a situation based on similar experiences that have occurred in the past.

When the COVID vaccine started rolling out, for instance, experts could estimate the kinds of misinformation that were likely to come out because of a vaccine misinformation playbook. This playbook is just a pattern of doubts people are likely to have about a vaccine, which turns into misinformation as people spread these doubts online. The CDC has a whole page of facts debunking misconceptions people have just about the flu vaccine.

So with fact-based prebunking, experts are saying, "I know people have said this for lots of years. Here's why this isn't true in this case either." Rhetorical or logic-based prebunking, on the other hand, is when experts tell the public about common strategies people use to spread misinformation.

"Misinformation often follows a playbook. The use of false experts where you try to pretend you're an expert, but you're not, or create an organization that sounds super official, but it isn't, are some examples," Vraga said.

So is prebunking or debunking more effective? The answer is: we need both.

A 2021 study Vraga coauthored with Leticia Bode, associate professor at Georgetown University, titled "Correction Experiences on Social Media During COVID-19" found the experiences of people "being corrected, correcting others, and witnessing correction on social media" regarding COVID-19 misinformation across both ideological divides were common (Vraga and Bode, 2021).

This is all to say one method isn't going to be enough to solve the problem of misinformation. What we need is an effective strategy where we outline what misinformation may possibly exist before it spreads based on previous narratives, and a system where we debunk misleading viral claims that are hard to predict.

Now I've given you an overview of the forbidden term fake news, misinformation versus disinformation, and prebunking versus debunking, let's head into the next chapter: types of misinformation.

CHAPTER TWO
MY FIRST ENCOUNTER RIGHTING A WRONG: "HE'S DEAD!"

The first time I distinctly remember correcting misinformation before I officially launched my fact-checking journey at two different newsrooms was when one of my followers posted the following on her Facebook timeline: "BREAKING NEWS: North Korean president Kim Jong-Un is dead!" I was casually scrolling through my Facebook feed when this message, which sparked over one hundred interactions, popped up.

I knew this message was false for one reason: no major news outlet had confirmed his death. Journalist Choe Sang-Hun reported for *The New York Times* in 2020 that rumors were circulating about Un's health, and the lack of information was causing people to come up with various notions as to what might have happened (Sang-Hun, 2020).

Surprisingly, my friend sent me a text of a screenshotted social media post that had a picture of Un in a bed with Korean text and what appeared to be a name of a nonexistent news outlet on a breaking news banner. But the image and the text, which I google translated, very clearly spoke to the rumor.

I immediately corrected both of them. I messaged the Facebook user who posted the message privately and gave her all the research I had done on the topic and texted my friend to tell her the same thing.

When I asked my friend where she got the image, she pointed to an Instagram page. The Kim Jong Un visual, along with a short caption, received over two thousand likes, which is more than the message on Facebook received.

That's when it struck me: the same claim was portrayed on social media in two different ways, yet both were powerful in getting the message across. People can spread misinformation through pictures, videos, text, audio, and links, but a combination of these mediums often makes the falsehoods they spread appear to look credible.

From what I've seen, images and videos tend to be more persuasive since these mediums not only speak to a larger audience but bring out stronger emotions as social media users are seeing firsthand what is happening rather than just reading about it online. People will say these mediums almost serve as "proof" the event is happening. And if we are thinking about these mediums in the misinformation context, that is typically never the case.

A 2020 study titled "A Picture Paints a Thousand Lies? The Effects and Mechanisms of Multimodal Disinformation and Rebuttals Disseminated via Social Media" digs deeper into this concept. Researchers Michael Hameleers, Thomas Powell, Toni Van Der Meer, and Lieke Bos brought up the concept of a "multimodal environment," in which a combination of images and text with misleading elements that surface on social media are persuasive to users (Hameleers, Powell, Meer, and Bos, 2020).

The most common example of a multimodal environment I've come across on Facebook is when a poster shares a long caption about five or six paragraphs long and a graphic that accompanies the text. The graphic may be one sentence that summarizes the caption along with pictures or a chart that depicts a trend the poster is referring to.

One time, a social media user posted a long description of how pumpkin seeds were effective in removing parasites from the body. They had about three blocks of text emphasizing a compound these seeds had called cucurbitin. The picture that went along with the post was the central claim, along with images of worms coming out of apples.

The image went so viral if you typed in Facebook's search bar "pumpkin seeds have a substance called cucurbitin that kills parasites in the body," a million posts would come up just with that graphic and caption. The information was false, according to a fact-check I wrote on December 13, 2021, but it was widely circulated.

Audio is also becoming a powerful medium in the world of misinformation. We've seen conservative commentator Joe Rogan's podcast on Spotify gain over a million views per episode. According to a list compiled by Edison Research, a consumer and market research company, in August of 2021 Rogan's podcast became the most listened to podcast that year (Edison Research, 2021).

This, however, is not without its controversy. Various news reports indicate artists such as Neil Young and Joni Mitchell have pulled their music from the platform because of the antivaccine content Rogan spreads. He has promoted falsehoods that urine therapy and ivermectin, commonly used to treat parasitic infections, are effective in treating COVID-19. I regularly come across fact-checks that debunk his claims.

By the way, please don't drink your urine or take ivermectin hoping it will treat COVID-19. It won't, and fact-checks indicate it is both ineffective and dangerous to your health.

Some good podcasts out there share accurate information about healthcare, climate change, and politics. Here is a list I listen to daily I *highly* recommend:

- **Beyond the RX**
- **The Healthcare Policy Podcast**
- **Columbia Energy Exchange**
- **Climate Conversations: A Climate Change Podcast**
- **The NPR Politics Podcast**
- **All Things Considered**

Finally, the good old beauty of links. Scrolling through my Facebook feed, I almost always encounter one of my followers sharing a link to an article or a website. From my experience, sharing links on social media and failing to present additional context creates many problems.

Reading a link to a URL and the small bio found underneath it and thinking the information presented on the website is accurate is human nature. I've seen this a lot on Facebook with the keto diet pill social media users purport Shark Tank judges backed. How these ads work is a twofold process: First, they share two images, one of a person before their weight loss journey and one after their weight loss journey.

These tend to be the promo images, which means even before the Facebook user clicks on the link in the post, they see the impact of the endorsed idea or product. Second, a caption is often supplied with the link referencing a popular figure with false claims they have backed or used the product.

As a college student, I was introduced to *many* theories in class. The one that stood out to me the most that could apply to this situation is called the Elaboration Likelihood Model, created by Richard Perry and John Cacioppo in the 1970s. According to a YouTube video uploaded by Michael Britt on May 5, 2013, the theory has two basic elements to it: central processing and peripheral processing (Britt, 2013).

Central processing is when a person focuses on the substance of a message, Britt explains in the video. In other words, they are scrutinizing information they come across and evaluating all aspects of it. Peripheral processing is when a person focuses on external cues rather than the message itself, such as the person behind the message or perhaps environmental factors, according to Britt.

A person can easily fall out of the trap of the keto diet pill if they click on the website link (which most of the time presents as a scam) and scrutinize whether keto diet pills are effective for weight loss. That would be an example of central processing.

Peripheral cues work a bit differently. On one hand, if a person looks at the images and decides to purchase the keto diet pill, that would be an example of peripheral processing since the person is not scrutinizing exactly what an advertiser's message is conveying. Likewise, a person could view the images and tell the ad is misleading, since most people can't lose up to thirty pounds in less than two days (it's also not healthy).

A person can use both central and peripheral processing to their advantage when encountering a misleading post. Making sure the caption of the post presents the facts, but also understanding *who* exactly is behind a message, are both important.

What I introduced to you was what I like to call the "broad model of misinformation." If we want to get into the specifics of misinformation, I couldn't think of a better model to direct you to than Claire Wardle's "7 Types of Misinformation and Disinformation Model." Wardle is a researcher for Full Fact, an independent fact-checking organization based in London.

She concocted this model after exploring the different falsehoods that spread during the 2016 presidential election between Hillary Clinton and Donald Trump. Here is what she established about the model, according to her 2017 article published on Medium titled "Fake News. It's Complicated." (Wardle, 2017):

- Satire or Parody: "No intention to cause harm but has potential to fool."
- Misleading Content: "Misleading use of information to frame an issue or individual."
- Imposter Content: "When genuine sources are impersonated."
- Fabricated Content: "New content is 100% false, designed to deceive and do harm."
- False Connection: "When headlines, visuals, or captions don't support the content."
- False Context: "When genuine content is shared with false contextual information."
- Manipulated Content: "When genuine information or imagery is manipulated to deceive."

These are her definitions of each category, exactly. I won't go into detail with all of them because the model is descriptive. The two categories I will explore more in depth are satire and parody, which are part of humor, and altered content.

HUMOR

Shannon Poulsen, a graduate student at Ohio University, told me she studies how humor can be a source, and *solution* to, misinformation. Let's start with satire. What differentiates satire from other forms of humor is the fact it seeks to criticize a certain institution in a comedic and sarcastic manner.

I don't think satire is exactly *bad*. I have a friend who is a political cartoonist and satirist, and she sees it as a form of artistic expression. Everyone has mixed opinions about what they read and consider humorous, which I won't get into. I think the most important thing to understand is whether individuals can detect what *exactly* is satire, and if not, how that can be problematic.

We've seen satire from the *Onion* and the *Babylon Bee* circulate on social media, but these articles can be very misleading for those who can't comprehend the humor the satirist was trying to get at.

"They need to just recognize it's a joke. When they recognize it's a joke, people are less likely to fall for satire," Poulsen said. By "fall for satire," Poulsen means people believe a literal interpretation of something satiric.

Let's take another example: an article published in the *Onion* on February 28 titled "Cancer Researcher Develops Feelings for Lab Rat While Working Long Nights Alone Together." Just from the title you can tell this is satire. I have a sister in medical school, so I know researchers must spend long hours in the lab. But someone who isn't familiar with that setting might not "get" the humor behind it.

So how can a person literally believe something that's a joke? Don't get me wrong, I've fallen into the trap of taking things too literally. Jokes are complex kinds of messages, Poulsen said. Most satire is based upon the incongruity-based theory, in which a person has to have two planes of knowledge and combine those planes together to make sense of what they are reading.

Let's take the popular joke, for instance: "What's the tissues favorite dance? It's the boogie."

"That's actually very complicated to get because on one hand, you need to think about tissues and colds,"

Poulsen said. "But then you have to remember all the different kinds of dance."

Not everyone has the knowledge resources that are needed to understand these kinds of jokes. It's also very different to encounter a joke in a comedy club versus in a social media feed lineup with a bunch of different sources and information, Poulsen said. That's what makes satire a much more complicated type of environment, as not everyone might have the political or scientific knowledge to understand complex humor. And when you don't understand it, you might think it's literally true.

Here's another example. I saw a lot of social media posts on Facebook circulating about how Alexandria Ocasio-Cortez said, "I don't need truckers. I get my food from the grocery store" in response to the Canadian freedom convoy protests, in which people were protesting the vaccine mandate the Canadian government placed on cross-border truck drivers.

People on social media copied and pasted the quote, acting as if it came from her. However, fact-check reporter Ciara O'Rourke from PolitiFact wrote a fact check on the quote on February 7, rating it *pants on fire* as the quote came from a satire website called Geniuses Times that claims it is the "most reliable source of fake news on the planet" (O'Rourke, 2022).

Can websites do a better job of labeling and defining satire? Possibly. But social media doesn't work like that. Users are prone to screenshotting headlines and parts of an article from a satire website without using appropriate labels or sourcing. This is an example of "stolen satire." And many people fall into this trap, believing it is real news.

In 2019, Poulsen conducted an interesting study with Robert Bond and Kelly Garrett, two communication professors at Ohio State University, about how much people believed claims made by satirical websites. It was published in The Conversation, a nonprofit news organization that publishes ongoing or published research from scholars, and on the Ohio State University website (Garrett, Bond, and Poulsen, 2019).

The researchers identified some of the most widely shared misleading stories on social media biweekly, according to the Ohio State University website. Then, they had participants in the study say whether they believed the claims in those stories. The results they got were mind-blowing.

Poulsen said Republicans and Democrats frequently believed in claims from satire sites. For instance, a graph on the website shows the top five believed claims by both parties from the *Onion*. Fourteen percent of Democrats and 9 percent of Republicans labeled the claim true "National Security Advisor John Bolton said that an attack on two Saudi Arabian oil tankers in the Gulf of Oman is "an attack on all Americans."

The study is still in progress and has not yet been peer reviewed.

So how can satire or humor as a whole help people fall out of the trap of misinformation? She conducted a study in 2017 with Dannagal Young, professor of communication at the University of Delaware, and Kathleen Hall Jamieson, the founder of factcheck.org, to investigate whether corrections were more effective if they delivered information in a funny way (Young, Jamieson, and Poulsen, 2017). They found video as a medium, whether it was delivered in a humorous or non-humorous way, "increased message attention and reduced confusion." So they didn't find humor was *more* effective. They found it *as effective.*

Fact checks come in the format of an article. If you've ever come across the message that says "independent fact-checkers say this information has no basis in fact" on Facebook or Instagram, you know your post was probably viral enough to catch the eyes of a reporter. A warning sign pops up on the post that says, "see why," and two or three links come up that have the organization's name listed and a fact-check article that was published.

"The challenge that fact-checking has is it comes after you consume this misinformation," Poulsen said. "It's not getting a lot of attention. People aren't excited, it's not a fun kind of information to consume."

The caveat with adding humor to fact-checking, Poulsen said, is fact-checkers may be seen as less credible due to their use of humor.

"I think these fact-checking organizations, they want credibility, they want to be seen as professional, and utilizing humor can be a detriment to reaching those goals, especially because there's so much disagreement with the validity of fact checks from certain political views," Poulsen said. "The moment we start to have jokes in there, people view it as inappropriate, not smart, not intelligent, etc."

But Poulsen said comedians have played an important role in taking humor and contributing to people's knowledge in some sort of way. Celebrities like John Oliver, Jon Stewart, and Stephen Colbert have solidly established they are not journalists and are simply comedians.

"Even if they're trying to throw stones to laugh, there are these positive outcomes in terms of knowledge and whatnot," Poulsen said.

Hasan Minhaj, who launched the show the *Patriot Act*, is a good example of this. In season six episode one titled "What Happens If You Can't Pay Rent?" Minhaj goes into detail about the impact of COVID-19 on eviction, which happens when a landlord removes a tenant from their property. The process usually goes through the courts. It was an eye-opening episode that taught me, a person who knows nothing about eviction, something new.

ALTERED IMAGES OR VIDEOS

Altered images pretty much populate social media. Someone takes a screenshot of an article or an image they find on social media, changes around a few words or adds in graphics, and shares it to others. I've seen two types of altered images on social media I like to call the "out of sorts TV graphic" and the "made up story." Let's explore these categories.

Almost everyone has seen a CNN or MSNBC broadcast with the news banner at the bottom and large text that reads *"BREAKING NEWS!"* Most of the time, the CNN or MSNBC logo appears on the news banner, indicating the news being aired is coming from a reliable and well-known company.

But what I've seen people do is take a screenshot of a live broadcast and manipulate it, so when people see the screenshot, they think the information did air on TV since the news banner and logo are present.

One fact check I wrote that was published December 21, 2021, is a good example of this. Ghislaine Maxwell, former girlfriend of convicted sex offender Jeffrey Epstein who played a role in exploiting underage girls, began her trial November 29, 2021, according to a 2021 article by journalists Tom Hays and Larry Neumeister from the Associated Press (Hays and Neumseister, 2021).

Epstein had a private plane in which he flew high-profile passengers. CNN aired a graphic that showed who six of these passengers were on November 30, 2021 on the broadcast "CNN Newsroom with Ana Cabrera." A social media user took a screenshot of the TV graphic and replaced former US senator George Mitchell's face with Canadian prime minister Justin Trudeau's face.

The "made up story" is another category I ended up debunking as well on November 10, 2021. A viral image of now billionaire tech entrepreneur Elon Musk as a child standing next to a robot was making rounds on Instagram. The social media users claimed the story behind the image was Musk built himself a robot named "Chappie" at a tech school he went to in South Africa.

The artist altered the picture; the original featured the artist as a child with two of his friends. He replaced his figure with the robot, though the story spread on social media was not real and unrelated to the picture.

Now that we've covered types of misinformation, let's get into our next topic of discussion: social media algorithms.

CHAPTER THREE
SOCIAL MEDIA INS AND OUTS

I, like many others, just *had* to explore the craze over the latest Amazon Echo deals that practically swarmed the Amazon site on Black Friday. Naturally, I logged on to my Prime account, scrolled through the products, and saved some in the cart. When I scrolled through my feed on Facebook a while later though, I saw it—*an ad for the same product and price listing that was on the Amazon site.*

It was no surprise social media algorithms were at work. In simple terms, an algorithm is a set of instructions a computer or machine is expected to follow. On social media, though, that can take a variety of forms.

If you identify as a conservative, for instance, you could get pulled into a lot of suggestions for conservative-related groups, and that's just the algorithms basing your feed off what you like and dislike. Algorithms can also target specific ads you've previously interacted with or related ads that somehow end up on your feed.

Social media algorithms have adapted to new technologies that make it easier for our data to be collected and used to a platform's advantage, but it can still be quite harmful when you think about it in the context of misinformation.

Harrison Mantas, former reporter at the International Fact-Checking Network and current city government reporter at the *Fort Worth Star-Telegram*, told me the methods of communication we use today are much more immediate.

"You have probably heard the saying a maximum lie can go around the whole world before the truth gets to put its shoes on. We've always had misinformation, but we just basically met the way we're communicating, that is adding the lighter fluid to the fire that was already there," Mantas said.

Social media algorithms have become a facet of misinformation because once a person watches a video or reads a misleading post, similar user-generated content will confront them. For instance, a person who loves herbal and homeopathic cures to relieve pain might be confronted with the claim almond juice can cure a person of heart attacks. Then, a series of posts claiming that different fruits have "healing properties" might follow.

David Rapp, professor in both the School of Education and Social Policy and the Department of Psychology at Northwestern University, told me pinpointing one specific source of misinformation is hard.

"It could come from anything. People learn everywhere, right?" Rapp said.

THOMAS HILLS, RESEARCHER ON COMPLEX INFORMATION ENVIRONMENTS

Thomas Hills, a professor at the University of Warwick, told me algorithms normally don't consider the quality of information and or have rules that specify the authenticity of a claim on social media, and that can contribute to the spread in misinformation.

"We already know misinformation is more likely to be valued and shared by people for various reasons," Hills said. "Algorithms share what people 'want' to see."

Cognitive biases typically focus our attention on social information, negative information, predictive information, and information consistent with what we already believe or look for, Hills said. Social media algorithms tend to promote things that are already clicked on by others, even negative and untrue content, and this can have a host of negative consequences, including overconfidence in false beliefs, negative outlooks, and hypervigilance to social information.

Here's an example. Let's refer to an example of a misinformation campaign around the Russian invasion of Ukraine, which happened in the early hours of February 24. A very viral video circulating on Facebook claimed to show an explosion in Ukraine after Russian forces invaded the country. But that video was taken out of context, and it showed an explosion that took place at a chemical warehouse in Tianjin, an industrial city in China in 2015. I debunked this claim on February 24.

The video was surprisingly viral; it appeared on TikTok, Instagram, Twitter, and Reddit. Because of the algorithms at work, people who you wouldn't normally think would consume the information did since it was shared and retweeted by others to such an extent. But that's how algorithms work: they lead us down a rabbit hole of beliefs.

Bots, which are algorithms designed to share information according to specific rules and often at very high rates, can also impact what we see and hear on social media. People in the background usually run these bots. Hills said bots produce a huge amount of information produced on Twitter since they tweet faster than humans.

A good example of a Twitter bot is the @NetflixBot. It automatically updates followers with posts when new content has been added to the movie and television show streaming service.

Hills researches how people interact with and produce information, including misinformation such as fake news and conspiracies. He's found people don't remember all the news they hear, but often mainly remember the parts that are most consistent with what they already believe and often that are more negative. I once spoke with a journalist who told me a source once asked her why the media doesn't highlight good news. And the truth is, it does. But because people tend to remember the negative news, that is what sticks in their mind.

He describes a phenomenon called information-learned helplessness, in which information complexity leads people to give up on trying to find the answer. You can see the phenomenon at work when misinformation is presented alongside true information. In other words, we may think something is correct if it "seems" too hard to understand, when, it might be a simple concept.

For instance, a lot of posts have circulated on social media that claim canola oil is toxic, and almost all the posts have been supplied with a "process" on how canola oil is made to provide evidence behind the claim. I saw a lot of versions that had words such as "free radicals" and "corrosive" product, which might make it seem like the process is complex. But if you did a thirty-second google search, you might be presented with the opposite case.

CHIRAG SHAH, RESEARCHER ON INFORMATION RETRIEVAL/SEEKING

I interviewed Chirag Shah, associate professor of information and computer science at the University of Washington, who told me his research has focused on social media and contextual information. Several years ago, he built a platform called Context Minor on the idea if a person tries to understand an object like a video or tweet, they need to understand the surrounding context, like who is using it and how.

"I believe a lot of the misinformation problems can be solved if only we were presented with the larger context behind an issue and are able to think beyond just that headline, or the tweet," Shah said.

Lately, however, his work has revolved around search and recommender systems, which create feeds and recommend content tailored to a person's tastes on social media, and its relationship to the "filter bubble."

A "filter bubble" is what happens when a person is continually obtaining information that reinforces their beliefs and creates this vicious circle of bias.

"One of the things I work on is called 'explainability' in recommender systems. That means a lot of these systems are black boxes in that they're doing something behind the scenes that even those who are seasoned users or are developers can't even understand," Shah said.

One of those "behind-the-scenes" ideas is how that algorithm is making these recommendations, habits, and resurfacing old beliefs, which are often coveted from the public. It's a little bit more nuanced than providing context, Shah said.

"If all of us keep propagating the same fake news, context is not necessarily going to help because it's going to say, 'So and so you like used it in this context.' And you'll say, 'Well, I trust that person. So that must be good.' Maybe the other side of the equation is from the system side because the system provides you with this explanation about why it's recommending something," Shah said.

"Algorithms are also tuned on optimizing user engagement, which on the surface may seem like a good idea," Shah said. As a professor, he said if he's teaching a class, he would want his students to stay engaged. In the real-world context of it, user engagement makes sense. But the way engagement works on social media is different.

"We now know for sure people are more engaged when they react more strongly to certain emotions, specifically, their emotions of hatred, fear, right conspiracies," Shah said. "And because of that, the content that portrays those emotions gets a lot more engagement. The algorithms don't see something being engaging because it is an important, interesting, and validated alternative, versus something being engaging because it carries those negative emotions."

The question of the hour: can we ever change that?

"All algorithms are business driven. The more engagement, the more impressions, more clicks, more shares, more traffic, which all couples to more ad revenue and more data," Shah said. Nobody's sitting behind the scenes at Facebook or Google and manually manipulating these things, he added.

These black boxes are designed for self-learning. But platform creators can optimize other dimensions of utility, like relevance and quality and authoritativeness, besides engagement. In a practical setting, though, tech companies will not do that because they will lose profits. So, would engagement be better controlled if private groups were disbanded?

Shah said that everyone should have the right to privacy, no matter how wacky the content they share is. It all aligns with ethical issues, too. For instance, if there's a group planning an insurrection on a government building, that could pose dangers to the whole nation, and that's where he said regulations could be useful. The debate on who will enact the regulations and how it will work, however, is controversial.

Action should be taken on our parts too. Shah said as an educator, he sees a responsibility to bring awareness and teach others about what to do when they are scrolling through their feeds and come across a misleading post. A cultural shift needs to happen, and it is nothing new.

"Think about big tobacco. We've done that before where we started putting these warnings on all the packs of cigarettes showing that it can kill you," Shah said. "Now you can still smoke, and people still do. But the warnings help people slowly come to a realization it is harmful."

FILIPPO MENCZER, RESEARCHER OF INFORMATICS AND COMPUTER SCIENCE

Filippo Menczer, a distinguished professor of informatics and computer science at Indiana University, told me the cost of producing, spreading, and sharing information is lowered as everything takes place on free social media platforms. That means the "gatekeeping" role of the media has diminished as algorithms determine what a person sees and hears.

Menczer's research has focused on echo chambers, a loaded term that means different things to different people. Some researchers, especially in the communication area, see echo chambers as an instance in which a person literally is not exposed to some information at all. The person may be completely unaware of certain news or facts.

He likes to describe an echo chamber as a social media community where there is both *polarization* and *segregation.*

Polarization means people connected to you are similar to you. There is not a breadth of opinions, as opinions tend to be concentrated and similar to yours. Segregation means the network itself and most of your connections come from that group, and very few connections come from other groups.

This doesn't mean you're not exposed to facts and information, but rather how you're exposed to them and how they reach you is highly modulated by this community structure, Menczer said.

"I might see the article from the *New York Times*, for instance, if I'm in a conservative chamber, but it will probably come through somebody who is saying something about it. And that person who is commenting on that article is another conservative person," Menczer said. "So it will be filtered through the lens of my own community that is similar to me. I may have access to all information, but access is mediated by that group."

Completely isolating from a source is difficult today. Research suggests even very partisan people, both conservative and liberal, are highly aware of activities, news, and claims about the other group, but their awareness is very biased, Menczer said.

"A conservative may know about the liberal legislation initiative or vice versa, but they may mischaracterize it. Or they may be exposed to that information in a way that mischaracterizes it," Menczer said. "So it's not so much that you're completely insulated from opinions or facts related to the other group, but you don't access that information in a way that is objective."

One of Menczer's research studies was based on a theoretical model, where he built a system that simulates a social media system. In the system, it was assumed that the platform, in some cases, could measure quality.

"For example, some platforms know when a piece of information is coming from a low credibility source or high credibility source. They also can see who is interacting with this piece of information, who is sharing it, and how many people are sharing it and liking it," Menczer said. "These popularity signals measure of how many people are engaged."

The system also assumed the platform uses a combination of the quality signals and the popularity singles to rank posts on a person's feed. Social media users don't see everything because they have limited attention. Therefore, they're more likely to be exposed to the posts that are ranked at the top by the algorithm.

"What we found is in general, the more weight the algorithm gives to popularity, the lower the overall quality of the information in the system," Menczer said.

In this model, however, there was no sophisticated accounting for factors like what makes something engaging. It could be that it leverages a person's emotional response and makes them angry. It could also be a case of confirmation bias, where a person is more likely to share things that reinforce their beliefs.

"So initially something may become popular, and the algorithm latches on and amplifies that initial signal. Whatever happens to be popular initially, then, is seen by many people because of the algorithm and more people are likely to engage with it simply because they see it," Menczer said. "So exposure itself leads to further engagement. This is a vicious loop, and in the end, a lot of stuff that was not so high quality initially gets amplified by the algorithm and spreads."

Menczer has also done research on social bots, automated accounts that may spread misinformation. However, they do not necessarily have to act independently. They could also be inauthentic in the sense one single entity can control many of them and can impersonate people. Platforms have become more aggressive in taking down suspicious accounts and accounts that are likely automated. But certain actors still use software, such as application programming interfaces, to interact with a platform programmatically through code.

"That means I can still manipulate people, because people get the impression they're interacting with different humans, whereas there is a single actor that actually controls them," Menczer said. "So this, to me, is a kind of social bot that is not autonomous, but nevertheless can manipulate people online."

What are some strategies these actors or bots use to spread misinformation *and* go viral? One technique Menczer observed early on is the targeting of an influential person who will get the impression many people are talking about something and will repost that particular message.

"Let's say I target Robert F. Kennedy Jr., who's an antivaxxer with many followers on social media. If I want to spread a particular piece of antivax misinformation, I can create twenty accounts, have all of them mention Kennedy, and follow and interact with him," Menczer said. "Then I tweet the CDC is secretly injecting a substance that controls your brain. If this person retweets it, this message is likely to go viral."

Menczer gives a real-life example of this with former president Donald Trump. An author at InfoWars, a far-right conspiracy theory page owned by Alex Jones, wrote an article claiming Clinton won the popular vote in the 2016 presidential election through fraudulent votes. Menczer found social bots that often replied to news sources mentioning Trump with a link to this fake article. Trump might think multiple news sources were sharing the claim since it was tweeted more than a hundred times. Trump did in fact restate the false claim.

The other strategy Menczer observes is flooding, which happens when bots repost the same thing multiple times throughout the day and crowd out information coming from reliable news sources. Some time ago, Twitter put a limit on the number of posts a person can have throughout the day to 2400. And now Menczer is finding accounts that can evade that limit by posting a certain number of tweets, deleting them, and posting them again.

When actors use flooding, they can trick the algorithm by making it seem as though a post is popular, and the algorithm will show that to more people. Flooding is essentially a reinforcing loop.

Finally, actors can hack the cognitive biases of humans. We tend to believe things that come from more people. Bots can create the appearance a lot of people are talking about a topic. So this is an interesting system where the bias of the brain combined with the bias of the algorithm create a vulnerability that can be exploited by inauthentic accounts.

Detecting whether an account you interact with or follow is a bot is quite difficult. However, tools developed by Menczer's lab consider several factors:

- The volume of content posted
- The profile
- The networks of friends and followers.
- The networks of retweets.
- Structural features of these networks.
- Emotional features extracted from posted content
- Word analysis of the content (Do they use more adjectives or verbs?)
- Temporal features (Do they tend to tweet at regular intervals?)

Menczer worked on a project he called "Truthy" in early 2010 to 2014 where he explored the diffusion of information on social networks, including nuances such as who retweets whom and the structure of these networks themselves, to recognize certain patterns that are characteristic to misinformation. Part of this project included storing a collection of tweets to look for similarities and differences between potential bots.

"The very first system we built was a website where you could look at hashtags and build the diffusion networks with these hashtags," Menczer said. "And then you would use simple machine learning algorithms to detect whether there is any suspicious activity coming from these accounts. You could actually look by hand to see who the influential actors were. That website was called Truthy."

In 2014, the Truthy came under attack from certain political conservatives who claimed it was an attempt by the Obama administration to silence free speech. He said his group who worked on the project were also some of the earliest to detect misinformation was asymmetrical, meaning conservatives tended to spread misinformation more those of other political ideologies.

So what are some solutions to reducing misinformation on social media?

Menczer said the cost of spreading misinformation has been reduced due to social media. One important thing to note here is "cost" doesn't necessarily pertain to money. It can pertain to time, limit, characters, and features.

Twitter gives someone the right to share 2,400 posts a day, but if they limited the number to five posts a day, that would increase the cost of spreading misinformation since a person's post volume is limited. That would also encourage someone to look at information before they reshare it. A limitation of this model would be legitimate journalists would also be limited in spreading information.

Another solution would be to put a price on communication, which would thereby increase the quality of communication. If someone wanted to post more than five tweets a day, they would have to pay for it. In some sense, this would be helpful, though it would again place people who do spread accurate information in a limited setting. Rich folks who regularly spread misinformation, however, have the money to pay for communication.

Because of these limitations, the solution to reducing misinformation using social media is still being studied. Let's move on to the next chapter: video games and conspiracy theories.

CHAPTER FOUR
VIDEO GAMES AND CONSPIRACY THEORIES: HOW ARE THEY RELATED?

When I was in middle school, I was addicted to *Wizard101*, a computer game that lets a user create an avatar who is tasked with completing a series of quests that lead them into dark tunnels, magic buildings, and different realms. The most powerful part of the game was it always led me on, even in ways I didn't know. For instance, the player sometimes had to pay money to fulfill quests. But to make sure users wouldn't leave, the creators had alternate tasks ready at hand that basically whispered "If you don't complete this, the entire wizardry civilization will collapse. Their fate is in your hands."

Seeing the spiral in which the game worked was interesting, and that spiral is somewhat like what we see in how conspiracies unfold. I sat down with two video game creators who have spoken in the past about the similarities between both.

I interviewed Reed Berkowitz, director of an educational game-creating company called the *Curiouser Institute*, who told me conspiracy theories in his mind aren't exactly theories, but fiction. He brings up this concept with the idea of advertising, and how both conspiracies and video games entice people to "buy" their content.

"It's very easy to merge them together. In some ways, anything you can do with advertising, you can do with propaganda, right? So video games are often used for advertising," Berkowitz said. "For example, the armies created video games to bring in recruits."

Conspiracies use the same type of advertising. Someone comes up with a grand notion something is going to happen and tries to attract as many people as possible to believe in it. Similarly, in all good video game design, a person always follows breadcrumbs.

Berkowitz said the purpose of the breadcrumbs is because video games don't necessarily treat the user as a detective who can solve crimes. So whether a person is playing a video game or doing a puzzle, everything is 100 percent solvable, and the game leads the player to the answer deliberately.

<block-quote> They're set up. The answer is obvious once you arrive at it. And of course, it's very satisfying. You're trying to set up that epic win. There are a lot of video games that are kind of detective-based video games, but it's really the same arc that you're trying to provide for the user in different ways.

For instance, Berkowitz said he played a game where a boy was missing, and he had to help the family find the child. The game provides all these clues, but the clues aren't of a real situation, in a sense. They're mysterious and interesting, as opposed to "Oh, he's with his friend. They took off for a day to go to the city."

"There are these weird coins and strange ciphers and puzzles and it's all to incite the imagination," Berkowitz said. "Also, problem solving in a big group of people is really fun."

We've seen the same thing with QAnon, where "Q" and his followers leave these breadcrumbs that the former secretary of state and presidential candidate Hillary

Clinton will get arrested, or former President Donald Trump will be inaugurated on January 20 and gain control of the "deep state."

The difference with conspiracies, though, is these things don't happen, unlike video games where users can see the events unfolding. So when a group of people entice others into their conspiracy, it is more powerful in the sense that people will always follow a trail of breadcrumbs they think will "eventually" lead to the desired goal.

> It's like when you are driving. You haven't asked for directions, and you keep going down this road and being like "Nope, it's got to be just around this next bend. It's going to be just around this corner, like we're going the right way," You're thinking, "Oh, it's so far to drive all the way back if I made a mistake; it's got to be here."

Berkowitz's research has focused on the term apophenia. According to Merriam-Webster, it means, "The tendency to perceive a connection or meaningful pattern between unrelated or random things." It is the opposite of epiphany, Berkowitz said.

> So you have an epiphany on one hand, which is arriving at a correct and useful truth, and then you have apophenia, on the other hand, which is arriving at a delusion that feels like you're arriving at the truth. So, a person would feel like something's going to happen and then they have this aha realization, and everything would feel kind of charged and magical.

For example, when someone hits apophenia, they think *I know what it is. I am an alien. I have been put here to gather information, and they're coming to see me back soon.* They arrive at that thing that makes everything feel right, even though it is wrong.

When you play a game, you want users to arrive at a specific conclusion and have that epiphany of like "I get how it all ties together. It's like clockwork. You're such a good game designer." But what often happens is they put two and five together and get two again. And you're like, what just happened there? So they misread your clues.

It's people jumping to a conclusion that isn't the intended conclusion, which is apophenia at work. Berkowitz gives an example of this.

If you're a dungeon master in a game, and you set up the game where the users have to solve a riddle that will get them to the City of Microdose. What happens instead is they read the riddle, and they think *I know what we have to do. We have to go to the pub.*

Apophenia's and epiphanies make a person feel good, so when a person has them, they get a dopamine hit. That's supposed to be there because humans are supposed to be curious. They're supposed to solve puzzles, and they're supposed to get rewarded for it. But you also get that same feeling in a much cheaper way when you get something wrong, because you think you're right.

Conspiracies work the same way. A person follows the breadcrumbs, does research, finds relationships between things that don't exist, and comes to their own conclusions. The difference here is the aftereffects. When fact-checkers or journalists come along and say something is wrong, that person feels insulted because they're encoding the information they have supposedly uncovered with a dopamine rush.

"When someone challenges their thoughts, it's the same as when they're challenged physically, because it's considered a part of their personality," Berkowitz said.

PART ONE

Lastly, Berkowitz introduces the concept of symbolism in both video games and conspiracies. Symbols are semiotic signifiers, which are images, pictures, or phrases associated with a meaning, also called the signified. For instance, when you think of the word apple, you may think of laptops or iPhones for the company. In a more abstract sense, if a conspiracy theorist comes across an illuminati sign, they may think it is referring to a sense of authoritarianism, such as "Big Brother" from George Orwell's book *1984*.

The dangerous part is when we are associating symbols as if they were real. I think the freakiest thing about QAnon is that whoever's running "Q" has these weird pictures where they're wearing owls and bullheads, but they create a meaning for it that is different from the real meaning.

Adrian Hon, lead designer of *Perplex City*, one of the biggest alternate reality games, told me most of his research focuses on ARGs and their association with conspiracy theories. When most people talk about video games, they are referring to computer games for the PC, console games, such as the PlayStation, and mobile games for smartphones.

ARGs are a special subset of video games that try to mimic reality. For instance, Pokémon Go was a widely popular ARG game where the main player had to move around their house and outside to capture Pokémon—creatures with powers that can be found in the Pokémon TV series. I once went Pokémon hunting with my sister and was so addicted to the game I didn't come around until 9 p.m. I was pretty much lost in my own neighborhood.

With video games, you tend to be controlling an avatar. But something important to remember with ARG's that make it strikingly similar to conspiracy theories is you are the avatar in the game, Hon said. You are putting in the research, trying to find what you need that will lead you to your end goal in a game. Going back to the Pokémon example, there are probably a hundred websites out there providing "cheat sheets" on where to find the rarest Pokémon—often hundreds of miles away from your home.

In some ways, it's less of an active process because it feels like an activity where you're the person who is clicking through different websites and making notes. But you're not the only person in the world, whereas in a video game, you might be the only human in that world. So it's a different kind of experience.

Hon describes a concept called "This is not a game" that takes place in ARGs. It refers to how alternate reality games like to pretend they aren't fiction to preserve a feeling of realism and retain a suspension of disbelief, he said. A good example of this would be *The Beast*, a 2001 Microsoft game based on the movie *Artificial Intelligence*, a film directed by Steven Spielberg about a young robot who joins a human family and tries to gain their love.

Hon said *The Beast* was based upon clues people would find in circled letters on the back of movie posters and credit scenes which would lead them to websites with various other clues. Even though the whole setup was a game, people were so involved in it that it didn't seem like it was fiction.

Conspiracies work in a similar yet different fashion. Falsehoods lead people on, but there is typically no end to the conspiracy, different from a game. Deceit is hard to assume. The actor behind a conspiracy could believe in the content, or they could be using the content as a way to gain a following.

On his personal website, Hon explores ARGs and QAnon further in an essay titled "What ARGs Can Teach Us About QAnon" on August 2, 2020. He wrote when he designed *Perplex City*, he "tried mightily to avoid editing websites, a sure sign this was, in fact, a game. Instead, we'd fix it by adding new storylines and writing *through* the problem" (Hon, 2020).

Now, something to realize here with QAnon is Qs followers like to change the storyline, too. For instance, when Trump wasn't inaugurated as president on January 20, various news reports indicated QAnon conspiracy theorists had moved his inauguration date to March 4, instead. That time, it didn't happen either, as expected.

"Conspiracy theories and cults evince the same insouciance when confronted with inconsistencies or falsified predictions; they can always explain away errors with new stories and theories," Hon wrote. "What's special about QAnon and ARGs is these errors can be fixed almost instantly, before doubt or ridicule can set in."

And finally, Hon brings up the concept of social feedback. He said, people communicate to each other on all sorts of platforms like 4chan, HN, and Reddit where ideas can easily spread.

> When they are watching, let's say, a broadcast or show on Fox News or CNN and see the anchor speaking to the audience, they might say, "Oh this person looks like they're the same person as in this photo I saw thirty years ago." They draw red circles around them and share it with other people. If the person says, "I think you really got something," that type of social feedback is powerful because it is confirming a piece of knowledge the person thinks they have. To be told that what they're doing is important is valuable and dangerous. It's more specific than playing

a normal video game where you're shooting someone, and then you help someone out. That's just for fun. Whereas in QAnon, this is serious. This is politics. This could change who the next president is.

People, whether they believe conspiracies or not, want to think there is some kind of truth out there other people are not seeing. It's just the truth requires more than one resource for it to be validated. Consulting experts, looking at research studies, talking to people with firsthand verified experience, and reading articles from reliable outlets ensures you have the facts.

A CONVERSATION WITH FELLOW DEBUNKERS

I am a fact-checker. But there's only so much knowledge I can impart to you. That's why I spoke to other fact-checkers who have more experience than I do regarding what they've learned on their journey's.

Mick West is a British-American science writer; the creator of Metabunk, a website with his fact checks; and the author of *Escaping the Rabbit Hole: How to Debunk Conspiracy Theories Using Facts, Logic, and Respect.* In an interview with me, he said the main way people fall into the rabbit hole nowadays is by essentially watching some type of video online.

> If you interview people and ask what the origin story is, they will always point to a trigger for them, which is usually watching a video. For instance, videos about the coronavirus being a hoax have words like plandemic in it. And once you've started believing one thing, it can become very easy to believe other things. They start finding out like this whole new world beneath the matrix that exists.

PART ONE

The best conspiracy theories are the ones that last the longest, are the most widely spread, and the ones that get lots of new information, West said. That's partly why QAnon is very successful: there's a constant stream of new things to believe. For instance, a QAnon believer could falsely claim former president John F. Kennedy Jr. would come back in Dallas on July 4, and once that date has passed, they would make up a story: Kennedy faced a delay and would come on November 26 instead. This is just an example, but we've seen it happen.

Different personality traits make people more susceptible to conspiracy theories. A lot of them, though, are just normal things every person has, West said. One is the need for uniqueness and the enjoyment of feeling special. A conspiracy theory happens to fulfill that need for an individual.

The most effective tactic conspiracy theories use in videos is presenting information in a way that looks authoritative, West said. If you have a video by someone who is a doctor, that is going to be a lot more compelling to someone than a video of any man sitting in his bedroom. If you have a video with high production values, that also makes it look like it's more real.

> Long videos are quite effective. It's kind of almost like a hypnotic thing. So if you make a long video with authoritative looking people you find, like a few architects and engineers who happened to believe that 911 was an inside job or the two pilots out of a million who think that contrails are real or some people who are in government or former government who believe in QAnon, it's easy for people to fall for that.

West started Metabunk in 2010 as a follow up to a blog he did called *Control Science*, which was about debunking chemtrails. According to an article published by David Keith's Research Group on the Harvard University website, the chemtrails conspiracy theory was the idea the government was making aircrafts spray chemicals into the air. If you ever see a rocket launch in the sky with white puff following the tail of it, that is called a *contrail*. The people who believe in this conspiracy think the same white puff is a chemtrail (Harvard University, 2022).

> I just got a lot of people in the comment section of my blog who were interested in conspiracy theories and wanted to talk about them. I set up a forum where we could have conversations and it just expanded to cover a whole bunch of different topics such as the 911 conspiracy theories, false flag conspiracy theories, flat earth, UFOs, and coronavirus-related things.

West believes supplying people with additional context is crucial to helping people get out of a conspiracy. With chemtrails, you can share old books on clouds that discuss contrails that persist. And with 911, you can show talks by architects about the construction of the building.

"The knowledge system is very limited and kind of bad. Where they get their information from consists of a small number of things. So supplying people with that additional context is very valuable," West said.

One video West uploaded on Metabunk back on January 3, 2019, was a meta-analysis of what some people claimed was a UFO flying in Utah. Here was the context behind the video: there was a small dot in the video that flew at high speeds in-between one or two frames but seemed to disappear afterward (West, 2019).

West discussed the idea of "small object hypothesis,'" an approach to detecting small objects in a distance. When people had visited the same location where the object flew, they noticed a lot of bugs in the area, which could have been the object. It certainly was not a UFO though.

I interviewed Shane Creevy, the editorial head at Kinzen, a technology company that seeks to protect communities from online content, who said he has been working in the verification of online content since 2009. During the Arab Spring in 2011, he saw all sorts of different videos purporting to be from protests in Tunisia or Egypt, when it was from an entirely different region.

"I think the most common form of misinformation we see is information that's almost true or close to being true, or in fact, maybe even is true," Creevy said. "That information is then recontextualized and repurposed for the means of spreading false information. Sometimes that's not on purpose."

Compared to other forms of misinformation, Creevy said he has seen memes spread the most, and they often use this tactic of B-test marketing. On the fringes of the internet, people experiment with different types of memes and images to see what gets traction, what gets attention, and which ones are going to last long.

"The problem is with other misinformation, you often see platforms figure out a system whereby they can take down the content," Creevy said. "The really difficult challenge with memes is it's very hard for the technology to understand whether the meme is a problem or not."

With memes, the variation between the picture and the text is so vast you can have one picture which is not harmless whatsoever, and the words on it can change, and they could go from harmful to not harmful and not problematic. At Kinzen, his team is trying to help build systems that will help platforms understand the emerging threats on their platform, including the spread of disinformation and hate.

"I wrote recently for the Tech Policy Press about how so much misinformation work is focused on the English language and the United States," Creevy said. "And we have so many problems in Ethiopia, or Myanmar, or various other parts of the world, which have not been tackled or addressed by platforms or by researchers. That is a huge problem Kinzen is trying to solve."

I've seen a lot of pages where that has occurred. For instance, social media users were circulating an image they claimed showed one of the queens of Egypt. I saw that same image on five different pages, each in a different language.

Fun fact: the Poynter Journalism Institute provides training and access to fact-checking resources for organizations worldwide, and this program is called the International Fact-Checking Network. But some countries might still not have access to fact-checking organizations debunking misinformation regularly.

Now we've learned a little bit more about how video games and conspiracies are related, let's move on to our next chapter: the psychology behind misinformation.

PART ONE

CHAPTER FIVE
UNCOVERING THE PSYCHOLOGY OF MISINFORMATION

Understanding the intentions behind someone's behavior or thought process can be quite hard.

The way I understand it, intention is a plan to perform a particular action. Sometimes, there can be a delayed response, meaning the person doesn't perform the action until much later, but still has the intention to do so. I want to introduce you to an incomplete linear-modeled scale I've been devising for about a year.

The scale consists of three factors: intention, persistence, and delay of action.

- Intention: I already defined this above.

- Persistence: When someone clings on to that intention; in other words, they still have the motive to believe in the falsehood and spread it.

- Delay of action: While the intention and persistence are there, that person doesn't *spread* the falsehood until much later.

Here's an example:

Let's say a person thinks the vaccines cause infertility. They read a post online about it yesterday and had the intention to create a post to share to others reinforcing the same misinformation. However, this person doesn't spread the claim until two or three months later. We can guess, using my model, the person was still persistent in their intentions to spread the claim, but had a delay in action to do it.

This can work vice versa, too. A person can spread the claim vaccines cause infertility as soon as they read the claim from the other post. And in this case, their persistence would be strong but delay in action would be shorter.

You also have people who still believe in a claim but decide not to spread that falsehood, and that's where the problem with this scale arises. Other factors can influence the scale too, including family, politics, motivation, willingness, and whether a person *shares* misinformation as opposed to creating it. I'm still modifying some parts to it. To really understand a person's thought process or behavior though, exploring psychology as a *whole* is important. Let's go through an example.

On the night before New Year's Day, I distinctly remember watching the movie *Don't Look Up* after much persuasion by my sister and parents who heard good reviews from their friends. Almost everyone had been raving about this film on Twitter because famous celebrities like Ariana Grande, Leonardo DiCaprio, and Jennifer Lawrence starred in it.

The film was about how two astronomers, who didn't have big names, had detected a comet hurtling toward Earth. After reaching out to pretty much the entire population, including the president, and trying to convince them action was needed to deflect the giant rock before it led to humankind's mass extinction, no one listened. It wasn't until people spotted the comet in the sky they understood the dangers it posed.

At the end of the movie, everyone ended up dying, except for the few who escaped Earth just a few minutes before the comet hit and landed on another planet.

The film brought up two questions that were angling in my mind: Why did no one believe the astronomers in the first place? And were people really that misinformed about a comet's potential dangers?

The movie played beautifully into concepts involving the psychology behind misinformation, particularly three concepts that are so important to its study: social desirability bias, confirmation bias, and recollection judgment.

1. **Social desirability bias** refers to the need to fit in, and that can sometimes require a person changing their attitudes on a topic, according to ScienceDirect (Mathieu, 2021).

   The reason no one took the comet seriously in the film was because the public was trying to fit into what the higher authority, which in this case the president, was spelling out: that the comet wasn't going to harm anyone. The two astronomers were depicted as crazy for even bringing up its existence in the first place.

2. **Confirmation bias** is when a person rejects facts because it doesn't align with what they believe. Usually, this type of bias can be found a lot with politics, but it does work its way into science too.

   In the film, a majority of the public didn't *believe* in the comet, and that caused major forces to act at a much slower rate.

3. And finally, **recollection judgment** describes a person relies on experiences in the past to make judgments about the present.

   The last time a comet hit the earth dinosaurs still existed; basically, it is way too hard to tell whether something is going to happen if there is no recollection of it in the past.

These are just a few concepts; group identity, beliefs, environment, and other factors also contribute to the psychology of misinformation. Let's see what experts are saying about some of these concepts.

RESEARCH THAT HAS BEEN DONE IN THE FIELD

I spoke to Dan Romer, research director at the Annenberg Public Policy Center at the University of Pennsylvania. He said we must be careful by what we mean by misinformation because some people believe it, and some people act on it, and so the question essentially becomes, *do people really believe it and act on it?*

"People may think ivermectin is going to cure COVID, and they may try to get it and use it, either to prevent it or to treat it. That would be a use of misinformation. Because there's no evidence it works, right? So if people go out and buy it, that's pretty strong evidence they believe it," Romer said.

He said the next question becomes, *where do people get the misinformation in the first place?*

Believing in misinformation is a social act because it is not just you who believes it, according to Romer.

> [Believers] are hanging out with people exclusively like themselves who have similar beliefs and backgrounds and political preferences

and all kinds of things like that. So you get sort of encapsulated in an environment in which things that are not true are believed by the people around them, Romer said. "And when that happens, they can become isolated to corrective information. And so, they won't read fact checks, or if they see them, they may not believe them, because all the people around them support the misinformation."

Romer said a significant segment of the country is prone to believing conspiracies about the government. People who are prone to conspiracies and whose social environments are supportive of those beliefs are also more likely to start believing conspiracies and misinformation related to it.

Another important part of the conversation to include here would be the idea of "group identity." People want to be part of a group, so when they find one that goes along with their beliefs, they will stick to it and defend the identity the group has "assumed." This is also a form of social desirability bias. In terms of reposting falsehoods on social media, Romer said there has been some research on why people pass things along, though it is still being studied.

> I think it's a combination of: it's amusing; it's interesting, whether it's true or not; and other people passing it on because they really believe it, and they want to send it out to all their friends who also would be inclined to believe that as well. So there's a lot of motivation for that, some of which are not reflective of believing it.

David N. Rapp, professor in both the School of Education and Social Policy and the Department of Psychology at Northwestern University, told me a psychological mechanism goes along with why people continue believing conspiracy theories that have been debunked.

"Whatever we hear first is going to be privileged in our knowledge and memory," Rapp said. "When someone explains to me why something has happened, that's the first thing that is encoded into memory and learned, and all of my subsequent understandings of that situation and context are connected to that original explanation."

According to Rapp, that first thing about a topic is also encoded into our memory and is thought about a lot. It's repeated to others, and even when it's debunked, that original idea can remain in memory and still be retrieved problematically.

> What happens is if something is repeated a lot, it's easy to remember. And if something is easy to remember, it phenomenologically feels like it's true. So if I can easily remember something, it feels to me like it's more true than things that are harder to remember. So mere repetition can have problematic consequences, and this gets coupled with the fact individuals who believe conspiracies often focus on looking up information and talking to others who support those theories.

Rapp conducted a study with cognitive scientist Nikita Salovich in 2018 titled "Can't We Disregard Fake News? The Consequences of Exposure to Inaccurate Information." The researchers found people who were exposed to falsehoods faced confusion in determining whether what they came across was correct, even if they had the prior knowledge to label it wrong (Rapp and Salovich, 2018).

For example (this isn't part of the study), if I came across a claim that said, "climate change was false" and a bunch of false data was supplied with the claim, I might rely on the falsehood being correct even though I have the knowledge to say it is false.

I interviewed Steven Sloman, cognitive scientist at Brown University, who said a lot of the effect of misinformation is not to convince people of something they didn't know, but rather to reinforce the beliefs they already have. In that sense, he said it's important to think about the various aspects of misinformation; not just what information is being spread, but how it makes people feel.

> The reason misinformation is so prevalent is because when you're making stuff up, you can make up stuff people like or outrageous stuff that is contemptuous of other people. And these are the kinds of things human beings are very responsive to.

In other words, framing plays a huge role in how information is perceived. I've seen two different types of framing on social media. One is the phrase, "Stay woke," which almost gives a sense of urgency to users they are living a fake reality. The other is using captions in all caps that make the social media user look like the expert authority when they are not.

I've also seen symbolism at work. Rather than supplying images with captions, sometimes social media users will pin three images close together and act as if there is some sort of connection. One time on my feed, I saw a follower post an image of an eyeball, an illuminati sign, and a sun together. I had no idea what it represented, but they were tying it to some conspiracy.

Other than that, Sloman said people remember things that fit their worldview. When people are told something they already expect to happen, whether it's true or false, almost serves as a form of justification the information is correct. Confirmation bias feeds memory in this case.

In terms of conspiracy theories, Sloman said QAnon's setup was quite ingenious. We will touch more on QAnon in the next chapter, but it was created by a mysterious person or group of people who call themselves "Q."

"QAnon was designed as a video game where people search for information, and they think they're searching all by themselves, and they're taught they're independent investigators, when in fact they're really just searching for information in some sense has been planted, and is waiting for them," Sloman said.

Sloman said he is not sure whether they trust Q so much as they're completely engaged and immersed in the process Q has set up. In terms of believing strangers versus experts, people will say they trust experts for the most part. Sloman's book goes further into this concept.

"Think about the days when we were hunter gatherers, we were literally dependent on the members of our tribe, right? Like, they might have been the hunters or the people who cook the food or the healers or the people who took care of the animals or right, like everybody had these critical roles," Sloman said. "And without those other people, we would be alone in the forest, and would die."

"What we're learning today is we're not just tribal in the sense we depend on others to provide resources. We also depend on others to think for us because the world is too complex for us to figure it all out ourselves," Sloman said. "That's why experts in different domains exist—to do that little bit of thinking and research for us."

The issue arises when experts are dealing with something they already have a fixed belief in.

When the expert comes and says, "Actually, you're wrong, the truth is something else." Now they must weigh their own community against that point. That's how Q and other conspiracy theorists gain credibility in the system.

> What's clear is our sense of community often dominates. You can say the expert is self-interested, or the expert is arguing outside of their domain—their true knowledge base. I mean, when you talk to climate change deniers about the fact that 94–97 percent of scientists believe climate change is anthropogenic, they'll say it's because the scientists have all this grant money for making that claim. So like, they have an excuse; they have a way of dismissing the experts' perspectives.

Finally, Jolanda Jetten, Dutch social psychologist at the University of Queensland, told me her research focuses on what happens to a person's social identity when they succumb to misinformation. Rather than taking a personality approach in exploring whether some people may be more prone to conspiracy theorizing, which may very well be true, Jetten says she studies how group dynamics and intergroup process on identity, particularly using an "us-them" approach.

> If you have hostility between groups, there's often quite a lot of cohesion within the group. When it comes to misinformation, both dynamics are quite important. Within the group, we're uncritically accepting the views of other group members without double checking them. Particularly in the case when we feel there's an enemy out there, we have to stand together in solidarity.

Polarization can play a role in strengthening this us-them mindset, according to Jetten. Everyone has their own beliefs, whether that be what political party they support or what platforms they stand for. Jetten refers to a term called "mudslinging," which are attempts to discredit and put down a different party. When a person joins a group that continually reinforces these beliefs, the person feels more empowered to be stuck in their own bubble, a process known as polarization.

"People tend to be influenced by others who have authority or seem credible," Jetten said.

For instance, when Olivia Rodrigo came to the White House in 2021 to persuade younger folks to get vaccinated, I saw people sharing about her appearance on Twitter and Instagram with messages like "I'll definitely get vaccinated for you." When Ariana Grande convinced people to vote on her Instagram while also providing places to polling stations, more than millions of her followers did exactly that.

Stereotypes, which are generalizations people make about others, divide groups further. People see their group as more competent and more intelligent than other groups, especially if polarization levels are high.

> It's a bit contradictory in many ways. High levels of competence are being attributed to those who are doing all of the dirty work and plotting in the background. At the same time, you think about all the conspiracies, even classic ones, like JFK (John F. Kennedy) supposedly murdered by the FBI, or the Twin Towers collapse being orchestrated by the CIA.

The last concept Jetten introduces is everyone has psychological needs they need to fulfill. In fact, I think Abraham Maslow's "Hierarchy of Needs" does a good job putting forth what some of these needs may consist of. According to the Corporate Finance Institute, the hierarchy consists of physiological (basic survival needs), safety (security, health, longevity), love and belonging (friendship, family), esteem (respect, self-awareness), and self-actualization (a stage where you have not only become the best version of yourself but have helped others reach their potential too) needs.

Somewhere along these stages is someone who might have lost physiological, safety, love and belonging, or self-esteem needs, and this could have had detrimental effects on their vulnerability to misinformation. The falsehoods make a person feel powerful, but only for a short period of time and not in a good way.

The last model I want to introduce in this chapter is from Steven Hassan, a health counselor whose work has focused on mind control. In a June 1, 2021 interview with Rebecca Catalanello, PolitiFact deputy editor, Hassan explores this model titled "Influence Continuum from the BITE model" that comes straight from his book *Combating Cult Mind Control* (PolitiFact, 2021). The interview was uploaded to YouTube by PolitiFact.

BITE stands for behavior, information, thought, and emotional control. On one end of the continuum are constructive and healthy BITE traits for individuals, organizations, and leaders, and on the other end of the continuum are destructive or unhealthy traits, according to Hassan. In a nutshell, some of the healthy traits for all three groups include "compassion," "unconditional love," "checks and balances," and "informed consent," while negative traits include "hate," "secrecy or deception," "ends justifying means," and "preserving one's power."

Spelling out these traits helps one see exactly how someone can fall into the trap of conspiracies and falsehoods. Influence is powerful, and cults and conspiracies are both very different and somewhat similar, which we will explore more about in chapter six.

PART TWO

PART TWO

CHAPTER SIX
STORIES OF THOSE WHO FELL INTO THE RABBIT HOLE AND ACTIVIST EFFORTS TAKEN TO COMBAT FALSEHOODS

Disclaimer: None of the stories featured in this chapter express my political views. These are entirely the voices of the two women I interviewed.

The first time I heard about the QAnon conspiracy theory was on January 6, 2021, when a mob of people who believed the 2020 presidential election between former President Donald Trump and current President Joe Biden was a fraud, stormed the Capitol Hill. On that day, I was casually scrolling through social media when various videos popped up on my feed showing these rioters climbing the walls of our precious government building and denouncing reporters.

I couldn't understand how a group of people could be so driven by misinformation to commit such an act. Some of the people who participated were QAnon believers.

A month later, I was assigned to write an article about the conspiracy for the Media Diversity Institute, an international organization that encourages accurate and diverse coverage in the media.

I referred to two reports compiled by the organization and the partner's project called "Get The Trolls Out!" which helps fight hate speech and conspiracy ideologies. Qanon was started by the unknown Q on 4chan, an imageboard website where users can post threads and interact anonymously. The movement spread to platforms like BitChute, Reddit, Instagram, Facebook, YouTube and 8chan, according to the first report.

The mystery here is that, while no one knows who or how many people comprise it, Q has found ways to establish itself. For instance, QAnon followers say Q is a "government insider who had top access to all of the secrets in the White House," according to the article I wrote. Q is also considered a pro-Trump and anti-state idealist.

In the article, I outlined several key falsehoods that circulated within the QAnon community, such as a network of "evil global elites" trying to take down former President Donald Trump, pedophiles running a child-trafficking ring underground, the coronavirus pandemic being fake, and vaccines being ineffective.

What really struck me was how QAnon presented itself as a paradox. You have this figure on a decentralized platform like social media where not everyone knows each other, and through that, Q was able to gather a tight-knit mass following.

A lot of factors played into this, but what Q and his followers skillfully did was create this *common ground* using simple features like hashtags and private groups on social media.

About fifty thousand hashtags and possibly more were related to QAnon, but the most frequent ones that circulated on social media included #MAGA (Make America Great Again, Trump's campaign slogan), #AGENDA21,

#PLANDEMIC, and #GODWINS, according to the second 2020 Media Diversity report.

As complex as QAnon is, it is not the only existing conspiracy. Fundamentally, we as human beings have always developed out of the box explanations for phenomena we try making sense of. And oftentimes, these explanations turn into conspiracy theories, even if evidence suggests the conspiracy does not exist.

For instance, the rumor former president Barack Obama was born in Kenya has been circulating since *forever*. The "birther" conspiracy theory still exists today, with people circulating fake Obama birth certificates online even though his real birth certificate, which can be found on the White House website, states he was born in Hawaii.

I debunked this claim on October 13, 2021.

In a society like today where people depend on others for answers, understanding how people can fall into the rabbit hole of conspiracies in the first place is even more important. When I think "rabbit hole," I think of the children's book *Alice's Adventures in Wonderland*, where Alice falls into a hole that literally takes her into an alternate reality.

Conspiracy theories are no different. The more digging you do and the more energy you put into trying to find something that isn't there, the more you fall into the conspiracy. And of course, everyone has their own way of falling into the rabbit hole. But everyone has their own way of getting out of it too.

I interviewed two women who have much insight into why people fall into the rabbit hole. One woman's journey is centered around QAnon: how she fell into it and when she got out of it. Another woman's journey focuses on the activist efforts she took to combat conspiracies after attending an alternate music festival in New Zealand.

LENKA PERRON

I first read Lenka Perron's story in the *New York Times* (Tavernise, 2021). And then, I had to interview her myself.

Perron said the most important thing to understand is what preceded being accidentally introduced to QAnon. Perron was a mother of three. Her parents were immigrants from Yugoslavia, a former country in southeast and central Europe, and were part of the working class.

"I was working with the Bernie Sanders campaign [in 2016]," Perron said. "I had been a Democrat my entire life—born and bred Democrat union, middle class."

In 2016, Sanders and former secretary of state Hillary Clinton were the faces of Democratic party, while Trump dominated the primaries for the Republican party in the 2016 presidential race. The news Sanders lost the Democratic nomination meant Clinton would carry the Democrats through the general election.

Perron said she and others who were part of the campaign were in an "emotional state" after WikiLeaks emails came out involving the Democratic National Committee and Clinton. She said it looked to her like a lot of "wheeling and dealing and backdoor deals were taking place to push Hillary Clinton across the finish line."

"Nobody was talking about people living on poverty wages, the middle-class issue," Perron said. "And that's where we became vulnerable to conspiracies."

She noticed insidious content suddenly started appearing on the various Bernie Sanders Facebook groups she was part of. She said it felt like voices were saying, "I will tell you what else the Democratic Party is capable of," which began this trail of breadcrumbs that led her to QAnon.

"At some point these breadcrumbs lead us to [ideas like] Democrats are blood-drinking pedophiles. Like it got that crazy, but it happened so slowly and so insidiously,"

Perron said. "It's very small breadcrumbs that were built on each other. And before we knew it, we were in the rabbit hole completely."

Perron was absorbed in QAnon content for four months. After working her nine-to-five job, she would spend her time pouring over content on social media. She said QAnon wasn't really a "group she joined," but rather, content she engulfed her world in. Whoever wrote the messages also used a very cryptic tone.

"They made you feel like they were insiders in the government, and they had access to all this information," Perron said. "'Get ready, it's going to happen next week! It's going to happen here!' And they will tie in real events."

For instance, in 2017, the Hartsfield-Jackson Atlanta Airport faced a power outage due to an underground fire. However, Perron said QAnon followers made it seem as though the airport closed because Clinton was flying in and out of prison.

"They are dangling a very exciting carrot in front of you. Come back tomorrow to find out what's going to happen. It's going to happen, whatever the conspiracy is," Perron said. "You're fixated on it, and you want to come back and find out what happened."

During the time she believed in QAnon content, she felt frustrated. She recalls nothing a person said to her could change her mind. A fact-checker or reporter? She said she believed at the time they were a part of the corruption.

She also said QAnon had many ties to Pizzagate, another conspiracy that emerged in 2016. WikiLeaks uncovered emails between John Podesta, Clinton campaign chairman, and James Alefantis, the owner of Comet Ping Pong, a pizza restaurant in DC, about a fundraiser. In a nutshell, believers of Pizzagate circulated claims a child-trafficking ring was in the basement of Comet Ping

Pong. In terms of QAnon, Perron said followers would circulate screenshots of pizza owners with very disturbing pictures of babies to reinforce those ideas, according to Perron.

The big red flag for Perron was when she figured out nothing was happening. QAnon followers would often say both Bill and Hillary Clinton along with Podesta, would get indicted for their crimes, yet there was no evidence of that happening. Perron said she googled news of both Clintons and found them on a beach in Hawaii, while Podesta was giving a presentation at a college campus.

The other red flag was the group painting Trump as a hero who would stop child sex trafficking. Perron said she saw no evidence of that either. Eventually, she pulled out of the rabbit hole on her own.

"I started getting a sense I was being duped. I was manipulated; I was lied to," Perron said. And it took time away from family, from friends," Perron said. "It took away my joy, because I was a very frustrated person."

ANKE RICHTER

Anke Richter is a freelance journalist in New Zealand who set up a Facebook group with others called the Rabbit Hole Resistance. She also founded FACT (Fight Against Conspiracy Theories), a volunteer network that helps bust antivaxx grifters and influencers. She told me her journey started in an unexpected way: through attending alternative music festivals and spiritual workshops. Because of her personal connection to many new-age and self-help groups, and her work as a cult researcher, she said she was alarmed about the conspiratorial and pro-Trump narratives she saw popping up on social media since the early days of the pandemic.

Richter wrote an alarmist piece in 2020 titled "Conspiracy cults and the mental health pandemic" on the website The Spinoff and later an interesting article titled "How alternative festivals become platforms for conspiracy theories" on April 21, 2021. One of the musicians she wrote about was a Māori musician who regularly spreads misinformation about the COVID-19 pandemic (Richter, 2021). He spread falsehoods on how the Rockefeller family, known for their banking and industrial fortune, and the Rothschild family, a wealthy family that operates an office in Russia, are tied to some sort of "deep-state cabal."

I think what's interesting to note here is subliminal messaging. Richter wrote this misinformation could spread in places where people are celebrating and dancing, their hearts wide open. That's quite powerful. Or they are looking for some form of healing and want health advice but don't trust the medical system. Wellness influencers offer antivax advice through workshops and on social media while they peddle their products, like essential oils and supplements.

"There's one festival called Luminate. They are a very spiritual festival, and it was clear very early on in the pandemic their organizers had completely fallen down the rabbit hole," Richter said.

Some of Richter's friends from the festival scene came out with an open letter to Luminate that got widespread attention and was signed by some of New Zealand's top musicians and DJs. It kickstarted Richter's activism. Two Facebook groups originated from that. Richter told me that concern spread about what was happening in alternative communities that didn't see the vaccine to protect themselves and others. The divide in the country was really felt when the mandates started kicking in New Zealand.

"I went through this whole process of having to let friends go, blocking people, and taking a stance," Richter said. "You have to acknowledge why you're grieving, why you're hurting, why you want to do something about this. And once you move through the emotional part, then you ask for the reasons, and try and find solutions."

Her friends who sent the original open letter to Luminate decided to step up. Richter said she came up with the name "Rabbit Hole Resistance" and started a Facebook group as a support space for those who live with people who regularly spread misinformation, including their parents, kids, friends, and other family members. All sorts of requests would come into the group: "My partner won't sleep with me because I got the COVID-19 vaccine, and she thinks I'm shedding!" or "My mom is completely off the rails with this claim."

She said the aim of the group is not to mock or shame those who have fallen for misinformation, but to support each other in an environment that can be alienating and stressful.

The thing that fascinated me the most was how social media, while often labeled as a cause of misinformation, is also a *solution* to misinformation. When these comments come in, for instance, Richter said the group provides resources that help people understand how to help *others* come out of the rabbit hole. Sometimes, this can be simply sharing an article that has tips on how to communicate with others; other times, it means engaging in deep and fruitful conversation.

"It's a very respectful space, and you also have to also realize in New Zealand, we have a large indigenous population, so there's a justified mistrust of authority," Richter said. "They've been treated differently by the medical system. Racism is a fact, and it has consequences on people's mental health."

While education can play a role in helping victims of misinformation, people in the space clearly see far more complex factors are involved—trauma, personal history, and race. So the group makes sure not to speak from a place of privilege. FACT is also a network Richter helped set up. It consists of doctors, scientists, nurses, educators, filmmakers, and experts who are passionate about pushing back against harmful narratives comprising of misinformation. They don't hold protests in the street, but they work with journalists, write open letters, do media campaigns, and report pages.

Perron and Richter's stories show *anyone* can fight misinformation. Perron was inspired after she fell out of the trap of QAnon, while Richter's was inspired through music festivals. Both unique circumstances, yet powerful in getting warnings of misinformation across. Let's move on to our next chapter: what these stories have taught me, and what you can learn too.

PART ONE

CHAPTER SEVEN
WHAT THESE STORIES TAUGHT ME AND WHAT YOU CAN LEARN

Communicating with someone who believes in misinformation requires what I call a symbiotic relationship. What this means is that both the sender of a message and the recipient have to show a certain level of understanding and willingness to learn. I'll give you an example.

I regularly message most of my family members who live in India on WhatsApp, a mobile app that allows for international communication. Misleading posts get forwarded from group to group all the time. My aunt forwarded a video with text accompanying it that read, "This is the moon at the border of Russia and Canada at the North Pole. It takes about thirty seconds from rising to setting, blocking the sun for five seconds, and immediately setting."

The video appeared as if it were computer generated. In the video, the moon not only rose from a distance in a perfect sphere shape with tiny craters *visible* to the human eye, it also disappeared into the blue sky within fourteen seconds. In just a ten-second google search, I saw that fact-check reporter Grace Gichuhi from Africa Check debunked the video on June 25, 2021 with an article titled, "No, video of huge moon viewed from somewhere 'between Russia and Canada' not real" (Gichuhi, 2021). As I suspected, someone made the clip.

When I shared the fact check with my aunt and cousins, they thanked me for sending the information.

But I asked back, "Who sent you this?"

I wanted to understand how this falsehood could have made its way into my family chat. We couldn't track down the original post, though I was told variations of this message had been passed around hundreds of times.

Not all communication encounters are this easy. One factor that contributes to this is a disruption in the symbiotic process. Maybe the person sending the information gets easily frustrated or doesn't have a compassionate side. Maybe the person on the receiving end doesn't trust the facts being shared or the sender. Perhaps external cues—like family, educational level, or context—influence how well a person understands *why* something is wrong.

In either case, there are steps to get to an ideal symbiotic process. Understanding how to communicate with someone is the first. Lenka Perron and Anke Richter's stories in chapter six were not complete; today, part of their journey rests in helping others, whether they have fallen into the trap of misinformation or just come out of it.

EVERYTHING STARTS WITH A KERNEL OF TRUTH

When I interviewed Perron, who documented her story in chapter six, she said most conspiracies start with a kernel of truth. Then the people behind the conspiracy make up everything else. To the average person, telling what's real and what's not is very hard because of the quality of a video or graphic shared on social media.

In late July of 2020, the viral Wayfair conspiracy theory made everyone second guess the bedding company.

According to Perron, rumors spread cabinets, bed sheets, shower curtains, and other home goods were being sold as part of a child-trafficking scheme. Social media users started naming these goods and posting them on social media under the guise if someone spent thousands of dollars on that product, they would essentially be "placing" a child into potential child-trafficking.

Someone took the smallest kernel of truth—that WayFair is a home goods store—and spun it into something unimaginable.

"My kids were coming to me like, 'Mom, did you see that? You can buy a big cut cabinet for $15,000 to $25,000, but you're buying a child into sex trafficking. I'm like what?'" Perron said. "And they're looking at this Wayfair ad of a big cabinet named Jessica and it looks official, but the ad was all fabricated. It landed on our kids' newsfeeds on TikTok and Instagram because that's what they're on."

Here's another example:

I debunked a claim on January 18 "Silent Children," a documentary that was supposed to be about child trafficking and was abandoned in 2017, was canceled after four celebrity deaths. The claim was spun in a way the decision to stop the movie—the kernel of truth here—was spun into a conspiracy with four people who never took part in the film in the first place.

So how do you pull someone away from these crazy conspiracies? Perron said it often takes a person hitting their "rock bottom" to decide to step away from a conspiracy, and that can vary for each person. It is almost like stepping away from an addiction, and it is not something a family member or friend can control.

> What I do is, I try to get my loved ones—who are very much still into conspiracies—to remember who they are. When you get locked into social media, your reality has changed," Perron said.

"So I talk about any other number of things that bring us joy—get us to be connected. As soon as they start discussing anything related to conspiracy content, I redirect without judgment or getting angry."

When a person does hit rock bottom, they need loved ones to welcome them back without judgment. As a volunteer life coach, Perron helps people who have either been sucked into misinformation or are slowly coming out of it by helping them focus on their relationship, physical health, and career goals.

"People feel unsafe, and they feel angry. So you get to the root cause of what's really angering them without bringing up the conspiracies that were added to it," Perron said. "That's important. It lets them feel heard, and you can put forward suggestions around that."

A STATE OF VULNERABILITY

Diane Benscoter, speaker of TEDx Talk "How Cults Rewire the Brain," told me conspiracies and misinformation can sometimes start through manipulation. We discussed the psychology behind misinformation in chapter five. However, Benscoter digs deeper into this idea with cults—groups of people run on a belief system and usually headed by a charismatic known leader. In cults, the leader tries to take advantage of a person's situation.

"Everybody has psychological pain sometimes in their life, especially for young people during a time when they're individuating and figuring out who they are," Benscoter said. "There's a lot of that kind of disconnection and feeling like no one really understands them, and that's a very vulnerable time."

Vulnerable people are susceptible to conspiracy theories and misinformation because they are looking for *answers* to some type of phenomenon. Joining groups with leaders, whether that person is real or an unknown user on social media, gives them a shred of false hope. Cult leaders also try gaining power by taking control of a person's worldview or decision-making process.

"They try to convince them everyone else is wrong, except you, that you have kind of the corner on truth," Benscoter said. "It feels like you've discovered something no one else knows and to have someone to blame, whether that be the media or the government."

Benscoter uses the term "viral memetic infection," which are ideas that spread rapidly like a virus and make up the framework of psychological manipulation. We've seen this at work in social media where one falsehood with over one thousand likes starts taking on a life of its own.

"I never imagined this perfect storm of things would happen—the pandemic, technology, and the algorithms of Facebook all coming together at one time and causing misinformation to spread like it did."

"Winning someone's trust by demonstrating empathy and trying to get the person to understand the truth or the facts is an important step in pulling someone out of the rabbit hole," Benscoter said. In this phase, nonverbal expressions are especially crucial.

One of the most important psychology theories I've learned in my communications class is the Face-Negotiation Theory by Stella Ting-Toomey, professor of speech communication at California State University, in 1985. In a 2008 article, management consultant John Ng outlines the part of Ting-Toomey's theory which comprises of two dimensions of face: "positive-negative" and "self-other" (Ng, 2008).

The way I think of face is a person's image they are trying to protect. If a person has a positive "face-work," that means they want to be included and respected, according to Ng, but if a person has a negative face-work, that means they want independence" and autonomy. How does this play a role in communication?

When communicating with someone, I think we need both the positive and the negative. We need to give a person space to reflect upon what they believe in and where they might be going wrong, but we also need to make them feel welcome and give them a safe space to talk.

The other dimension is self-other. According to Ng, self means a person's attention is directed toward themselves. If they are in a tough situation, they try to "save'" themselves. We see this a lot in individualistic cultures. Other means a person's attention is directed toward someone else, meaning you want others to look good, even at your own expense. We see this in collectivist cultures.

I think this can go both ways. A person needs to focus on themselves by understanding the bias and attitudes they carry through self-reflection. Sometimes "saving face" doesn't just mean sticking up for yourself but taking a step back and thinking about how a falsehood would affect others. At the same time though, a person needs to care about how they react in front of others who do believe in misinformation. Would you be angry because that person thinks COVID-19 vaccines are dangerous? Or would you be sympathetic? If you spoke in a certain way, how would that make a person look or feel? These are all questions to consider.

The other theory, discussed many times throughout this book, is cognitive dissonance, which is the mental discomfort people feel when they are confronted with two opposing ideas. Developing psychological consistency, in this case, is important, and that can be different for everyone.

IT'S AN EMOTIONAL PROCESS

I interviewed Steve Eichel, a licensed and board-certified psychologist, who said a lot of ridiculous content on social media is shared because people are driven by their emotional processes and the groups they are a part of that essentially influence them.

Let's look at conspiracy theories and cults because the distinction between the two is fine.

The people recruited by cults usually fall into one of two categories. They are either seekers or they are sufferers. Seekers are very consciously deliberately looking for answers, according to Eichel. They can often be called hoppers because they go from one group to another looking for an answer.

"If the group isn't quite perfect, they leave that group and go to another group," Eichel said. "Those kinds of people wind up forming their own cult."

Then there are the sufferers, which is anybody who might be going through a hard time. The most common example is a college student who maybe feels a little out of place after moving from a rural place to a large state university campus.

"Or maybe it's someone who's older who lost their job or who got divorced," Eichel said. "In other words, they're in the process of some form of transition, and those people are vulnerable to cults."

With conspiratorial groups, it's usually people who feel disempowered who join and are encouraged by other members to believe the group has the real answers. The person feels special, and anything others say might drive them further down the rabbit hole.

"They become agitated, angry. They become very energized, and that's an important thing to keep in mind," Eichel said. "The people around them begin to kind of back away from them because they're angry."

Eichel said the first thing anyone should realize is they're not going to make an immediate change in someone else's beliefs. He explained there's no magic evidence that says, "Here's the smoking gun. If I just show the person that smoking gun, they'll realize they've been duped." A person is essentially dealing with self-fulfilling prophecies of circular logic.

Eichel used the following example about flat earth believers to explain:

"We're talking about space stations that can actively show the earth is a globe and revolves and orbits. That level of proof can't influence a flat earther," Eichel said. "You can take one of these people and send them to outer space and bring them back and they will say you manipulated them, and they never actually left the ground. That's the level of unrealistic thinking you're dealing with."

If it's a good friend or wife or husband, or whoever, the person needs to realize they are going to be in it for the long haul. But that doesn't necessarily mean no actions can be taken. The most important thing is to maintain a relationship with that person.

"One of my favorite cousins became an antivaxxer. One of my wife's nephews is involved with QAnon. With my cousin, I told him we don't talk politics. But we can certainly talk about a lot of other things. Like, how do you know the cup you're holding in your hand—how do you know that's a cup?" Eichel said. "Let's discuss the nature of perception. Let's talk about the vacation we took together and had a really good time."

Making the person feel disempowered and unimportant doesn't accomplish anyone's goal. So the most important thing is to introduce facts as you see them, very gently and over a long period of time.

"For example, you've got a flat earther. I would just say something along the lines of, 'Wow, isn't that amazing?

Bill Shatner, you know, played Captain Kirk all those years on Star Trek, he finally got to go and explore space,'" Eichel said. "What I'm hoping for is the person is going to think he went into outer space, and he's very clear the Earth is round. You know, why would Bill Shatner lie about that?"

With his wife's nephew, Eichel might say to him, "How do you know that earth is a globe? How do you know?"

Questioning facts a person already believes in is a good way of getting them to question the misinformation they believe in, since the same logic of presenting the evidence applies in both scenarios.

"I'm going to assume even most people who believe in QAnon believe we live on a globe. So what I'm doing is, I'm not asking that person to think about vaccines or Trump or anything else," Eichel said. "I'm asking them to think about how they can prove the earth is a globe."

In a decentralized world where most people communicate with others on social media, a person could easily think someone is similar to them because all they see is the surface-level of their followers. It's similar to a dating app, according to Eichel. People fall in love over the internet all the time and are willing to leave their husbands or wives of almost twenty years to be with this person whom they've never met before in real life.

"It's easy to say no to someone you don't know, but it's a little bit more difficult when you do know that person," Eichel said. "It's a little bit more difficult when you think that person is very similar to you."

QAnon's followers lure a person into their group based on what that person has in common with the rest of the gang. But conspiracy theories are also not composed of a homogeneous group of people, according to Eichel. Some people are so desperate to be a part of something that oftentimes no persuasion is necessary to get them to join a group.

"Imagine you're a car salesman and someone comes to your door. They already know what car they want, and they have to get one because their old car died," Eichel said. "How much of a sales pitch do you have to give that person? In fact, if you give that person too much of a sales pitch, they're going to walk away."

The last component Eichel introduces is the level of ambiguity a person can deal with, which often marks the threshold for whether they are more easily able to succumb to a conspiracy theory or believe a falsehood. That is part of the emotional issue, Eichel explained.

"Your personality has to deal with the degree to which you can tolerate ambiguity. There's an old saying if you're dating and it's a brand-new person, if they have to call you all the time for reassurance, that's one of the best ways to end a relationship, right? Nobody likes that," Eichel said.

For some people, ambiguity is difficult to deal with, and that can create anxiety. In talking with the anti-vaxxers, Eichel found one of the things they've said to him is, "Well, you know, last month, the Centers for Disease Control and Prevention said this, now they're saying something different." But that's just how science works. It is constantly changing based on new research and data through skepticism and the scientific process.

"I'll tell you a story I often tell my patients when they're struggling with ambiguity. I had a friend years ago named Jimmy. He got a job with a construction company to work on an LA highway," Eichel said. "Jimmy's backing out of his driveway one day, while a car is driving down that street. The driver of that car has a heart attack and dies while driving. His car hits Jimmy's car and kills Jimmy."

That unpredictability is what everyone faces in their day-to-day life, and unfortunately, the way a person chooses to engage with that allows them to move forward.

"Even if we tell our kids they are only allowed to drive within a five-mile radius, that's exactly where accidents occur," Eichel said. "My point is, we don't want to think about these things because we need to have safety. Anxiety over ambiguity, we all have it and we deal with it in different ways. Some ways are more productive than others."

CHAPTER EIGHT
JOURNALISTS' INSIGHT INTO BUILDING TRUST

The question of the hour: What do you do when someone doesn't trust you? We've all encountered situations where someone has lied to us or coerced us into doing something we didn't like. More often than not, the result was a level of trust we had with that loved one diminished to a certain extent.

Trust is a very complex topic, and it can take many forms. Maybe we stop communicating private concerns with someone close to us because we know they might spill beans to someone else. If a student did something bad in school, they wouldn't tell their teacher about it since the news might go straight to the principal. In a real adult world setting, that would translate to a suspect not confessing a crime to the police for fear they might end up in jail.

On social media, that might look like a conservative or liberal unfollowing a news media outlet because their friend or favorite political candidate influenced them to believe the journalists there are untrustworthy (yes, we've seen that happen). Peripheral cues can also diminish trust, both in person and on social media. If we see someone with tattoos, a muscular appearance, and an angry face, we tend to avoid them because we think they might be dangerous, even though we know nothing about them.

That looks different on social media. You can judge a person by their pictures, including how they present themselves, what type of captions they post, and how they interact with others. Trust is ambiguous and can be understood in many ways. Rachel Botsman, renowned author of *Who Can You Trust*, put together a nice definition of trust in her 2016 TEDx talk I think fits the bill.

She defines trust as a "confident relationship to the unknown" (Botsman, 2016).

"Now, when you view trust through this lens, it starts to explain why it has the unique capacity to enable us to cope with uncertainty, to place our faith in strangers, to keep moving forward," Botsman said in the TEDx speech.

Botsman illustrates this idea with the trust stack, which are common steps people take to "leap" into the unknown. These steps include "trusting the idea," "having confidence in the platform," and "using little bits of information to determine whether the other person is trustworthy," according to Botsman.

These two concepts are very relevant to the discussion of misinformation. Someone could post a falsehood on social media and people could take a chance in trusting what is being shared, even if they don't know who the user is or where the information is coming from.

How does a person automatically determine the credibility of a post? Identification is one factor. If a person saw the person who shared the post has the same beliefs they do, they will most likely believe what the person is sharing is the truth.

Other methods exist too. If a page was spreading misinformation, for instance, the person behind the screen could easily make up a logo or name that makes others convinced the page has credibility.

PART ONE

I think if you are a strong believer of the facts, one step to combat misinformation is building trust with those in your community. And who better than journalists themselves who disseminate information to the public every day to provide insight into how to build trust? Here are some key points journalists have offered on trust building:

TONYA MOSLEY

Tonya Mosley is an Emmy and Murrow award-winning radio and television journalist, who cohosts NPR and WBURs midday talk show *Here & Now* alongside Robin Young and Scott Tong. She told me examining the ways in which information-gathering has changed over the course of the past two decades is important to understanding how people gather the news. She said:

> Up until the last fifteen years, we have only had a few sources to choose from. We had our local newspapers. We had our local news stations. This is before the Internet became a thing. So with that, you just went to the folks you knew and trusted as a means of finding out information.

Now we have so many sources and other ways of getting information and people are understanding there is not just one type of journalism. Even so, Mosley said the role of a journalist should be to shed light in the dark corners of society, and that can be done in many ways.

> I think we are moving further and further away from the type of journalism that is just explaining an event that happened, and there is nothing else attached to that. But I will say we have really failed communities over the generations, especially Black and brown communities, and especially on the local level, because so much of the resource and emphasis has been this type of journalism."

According to Mosley, the principles of objectivity require you bring your skills and your way of finding out everything about a topic or person. Then a reporter takes what they hear and all the questions that come up with it, and they are critical of it in a compassionate way. To Mosley, this concept is part of the larger scheme of compassion.

> I like to call it being compassionately critical. You are passionately pushing back so that you can get a clearer understanding or better sense of the truth and then you go to test that. You find as many sources as possible so that you can document multiple sides to a story.

Part of this process also includes providing context. Giving the background on similar occurrences that have happened in the past and explaining why exactly something is what it is helps the other person understand the facts better.

Mosley says on air, she has to act as both a history teacher and newscaster because explaining an issue is not enough.

> It is what we see with politics. We have to understand how we got here. For us, that means providing people with the tools and the tools are the context. With that, we are weaving together a story that will go down in history. We are a matter of record which means we are recording what is happening in the moment.

ERNEST OWENS

Ernest Owens, editor at large of the *Philadelphia Magazine* and president of the Philadelphia Association of Black Journalists, told me he offers three key ways to build trust with the people.

First, he says he always has an open channel where individuals can give feedback or offer thoughts on news that has been reported that day. These channels can be through social media, in-person events, or even through email or text.

> I have always allowed myself to be accessible to people in some sort of facet. Whenever I tweet an article I have written, I allow my readers to reply to that tweet so that they are able to offer their perspectives. I also receive weekly emails from readers. That allows me to have accountability. There has to be some type of channel for people to share feedback.

Owens says journalists are supposed to speak truth to power, and they are supposed to do this work fearlessly, unapologetically, and ethically. At the end of the day, journalists are not responsible for making anyone look good or bad, he added, because journalists are truth seekers.

Finding information in ethical, meaningful, and moral ways, and distributing that information to the public so they can make meaningful decisions is the second method.

> What we do is take a mirror and reveal what we see. We often center our work around institutions that are accountable to the public at large because there is a certain level of transparency that is expected by the public from these institutions, Owens said. We give the people who are running these institutions our electoral votes, our votes of confidence, our taxpayer dollars to allocate, and a chance to represent and lead the public. With that much power comes much to be expected.

Sometimes, people don't know about the work reporters do, and that can also contribute to a decline in trust for journalism. There should be steps taken to ensure transparency in that matter, such as speaking at public events, encouraging news literacy in classrooms, and even visiting libraries which is the number one source of facts.

> We don't make it a point to collectively go out in these high schools and advocate for more curriculum that talks about the field—go to schools, meet kids where they are talking to people in the community and tell them what we do.

Being mindful of confirmation bias is the third factor. Owens said when people see something they like, they believe it, but when they see information that goes against their beliefs, it is automatically "fake news."

> One way to help reduce confirmation bias is to acknowledge what biases you have even before you walk into a conversation, or even before you read a fact check or article written by a reliable news outlet and try to keep that bias separate from what you are hearing or reading.

ROBERT HERNANDEZ

I think one big problem that contributes to why people fall into the trap of misinformation is they are not seeing themselves in the newspapers they are reading, and that can be quite problematic. Robert Hernandez, a professor at the USC Annenberg School for Communication and Journalism, told me the best way to combat lack of representation is to spend more time reaching out to, profiling, and pitching stories about a variety of individuals with diverse experiences and backgrounds.

> Look, you can either write about abstract numbers, or you write about one person, or you can amplify or do both a lot. Profile a lot of people, put

them on the front page. Putting them on the front page above the fold to say, this is an everyday hero in our neighborhood. This is who this person is and how they affect you and you affect them. To do that on a daily basis—you start to then collect that and get a sense of community.

Sense of community is important because the more people see trusted friends, family members, or acquaintances on the radio, on TV, or even in print, they will gravitate toward reading the news to gather information and engage in similar actions their community members are engaging in.

Another approach would be to pitch or write stories that reinforce everyday acts that support our society should be celebrated and amplified. For instance, having a community member be featured on the news for wearing a mask and saving lives during the coronavirus would encourage others to do the same.

So you get first representatives of the community that are valued and trusted to do the action you want the rest of the community to take and realize it's not one person that will influence everybody, but it's a variety of different people. Also, realize it's not one type of messaging. It can't just be printed in the paper, maybe you need to go to the radio station, the TV station, but also local corners, right?

Hernandez said when he worked at the *Seattle Times*, he and his colleagues put together a page on the website called "Fund for the Needy," where they would profile seniors, children, and families who lived in vulnerable neighborhoods in the Puget Sound region. Through their reporting, the journalists were able to raise money for local nonprofits to support those people.

There is an interest of people wanting to learn about their neighbors and to understand, to have empathy, and to see themselves there. And I think that's a valued approach to do that opposed to writing just an abstract thing.

STEVEN HERMAN

Steven Herman is a member of Voice of America's News Standards & Best Practices unit. He told me one technique in combating misinformation is to ask questions, regardless of what the questions are. Asking questions not only encourages you to be curious about the subject matter at hand, but it also leaves space open for wanting to *know more.*

In terms of building trust, questions don't necessarily need to be asked by a person or group of people you are trying to communicate the facts with. Sometimes, it can also be you asking the questions to those people about where the falsehood originated, how many people it has impacted, and so forth.

Herman said asking questions in a collected, professional, and concise manner is the best way to gather information. This comes from his experience reporting on two presidencies, five press secretaries, and being a VOA correspondent and bureau chief in India, Korea, and Thailand.

Herman likes to use the principle of brevity when asking questions in a very fast-paced environment. Herman, who reported on the Trump administration, said that getting the former president's attention right before he was about to leave on a trip was difficult as there was typically a whole crowd of reporters beside him wanting to start interrogations.

So he came up with the "seven words or less" rule, which made exchanges in those situations quick, easier, and straightforward because all his questions were kept to under eight words. He said he would decide whether to ask follow-up questions for clarification or create an opening for scrutiny and judgment. This is important because as you build trust within your community, you don't want to amplify misinformation, so ensuring you are as concise and clear as possible when asking questions or delivering information is crucial.

So what do you do in an interview with someone in your community or on social media spreading falsehoods? The word journalists love to use is *prepare.* Don't just walk into a conversation or an interview without already having planned what you want to ask.

Here are some of the ways I like to prepare for an interview or conversation:

- Think about the situation and what is happening. Where do you think you could get more clarification? What have you read online? Has any news outlet written about the issue? Who is involved?

- Do research, but don't come up with preconceived notions. You never want to walk into an interview unaware, but at the same time, you don't want to make assumptions or generalizations. Hearing their story and asking where the falsehood originated is important.

- When formulating a list of questions, ask both open-ended and closed-ended questions. I always use open-ended questions in an interview, but I do like to add in two or three quick close-ended questions to ensure I don't mishear or misquote anyone when I am typing my interview notes.

- Ask questions that clarify your doubts about a particular matter. Dig into the subtle nuances that the other party has mentioned. Look for and understand the context in which someone is giving you an answer.

- Have backup! We have so much technology, so don't just come in with a pencil and piece of paper. Have a recording device next to you or record your interview through your laptop.

When consulting experts, the questions may look different. You absolutely want to cover the *who, what, when, why,* and *how.* Some of the questions you can ask experts or reliable sources you are consulting include, but are not limited to:

- **The "is this source reliable?" direction**: Which sources are deemed trustworthy and credible for this particular type of information I am spotting on the web? Who do I need to consult if I come across information that can't be answered online? Is the source that shared this information trustworthy? If not or if so, how can you tell?

- **The "have those claims been verified by multiple sources" direction**: How many people have verified or debunked this claim? Who are we talking about? Do you know anyone else I can speak to about this subject matter who has also verified or debunked this claim?

- **The "expand a bit more" direction:** Can I have more context about what you are saying? Where are you getting these numbers from? This is what I currently know about the subject matter, do you think what I know matches up with the facts?

- **The "where is the evidence for this" direction:** Are there research studies out about this particular matter? What about other forms of evidence that show this is true?

These questions depend on what information you are looking for and why you are interviewing the person. Sometimes, you won't be able to use these techniques for every phone call you make.

Almost every journalist I have worked with in a newsroom also says right before you are going to end your interview, you should ask the famous question, *"Do you have anything else to add?"* This will almost always ignite a response, and you will most likely get information or quotes you didn't previously ask for. Now we know how to build trust with people in our community, let's head into our next chapter: social media tactics.

PART ONE

CHAPTER NINE
MY TAKE ON HOW TO COMBAT MISINFORMATION

I was on the phone with Greg Toppo, former senior editor at Inside Higher Ed, after I came across an interesting article published in 2003 by award-winning journalist Chip Scanlan at the Poynter Institute. The article, titled "If Your Mother Says She Loves You: A Reporter's Cautionary Tale" goes into detail about an interesting experience Toppo faced when he worked at the *Santa Fe New Mexican*, a local newspaper (Scanlan, 2003).

According to the article, Toppo received a call from a rather distressed woman on a Saturday afternoon, who told him a family member died in the Washington, DC area. She asked him if he could run a short obituary for the man in the Sunday paper. He agreed, so she sent him a hand-written fax a couple of hours later.

The next day, Toppo wrote a short piece about the man and read at the bottom of the fax donations should be made to the New Mexico AIDS Center. Toppo had never heard of the place; a quick google search proved the place never existed. The woman had also left no name or number on the fax.

Eventually, Toppo figured out through the man's ex-wife he was, in fact, alive. The man was dating two women, one whom he just broke up with living in Austin and another who was a "longtime companion" in Santa Fe. It turned out his ex-girlfriend in Austin made up the whole story.

"Never ever in a million years would I think somebody would be making something like that up," Toppo said.

The moral of the story? *If your mother says she loves you, check it out.*

The first time I encountered this famous journalist's creed was in a college class, and I chuckled because I thought w*hat a silly thing to say.* But the meaning behind the phrase, as my professor told us, is when we are confronted with information—whether it comes from a source or whether it is found online—we should check it out.

"It's very cynical but I think it's warranted because especially now, so many people are trying to pull one over on us. And for me, the worst sin is to be fooled," Toppo said.

So how do you make sure you don't get fooled on social media? There are tactics you can use to spot misinformation. We've been through a couple of them in previous chapters. However, here are a few new ones:

Reverse Image Search: This is probably the most helpful tactic. If you come across a picture and are unsure of where it originates, use TinEye or Google Image Search. All you have to do is copy and paste a URL or upload the image. Previous reporting done using the image would appear. This can also work if you take screenshots of videos too.

Statistical Analysis: Some posts on social media have numbers on them, but chances are, you probably don't know where that number came from. For instance, I remember seeing several posts that said seniors on social security received an average benefit of $12,000 in

2019. This may seem believable at first. But you should also do statistical analysis to verify. If you go on to the Social Security Administration website, you can get the salary range of retired workers in previous years. Calculating the average benefit of retired workers in 2019 amounted to a little more than $17,000 (so nowhere near the $12,000 figure).

Placing things in context: You've probably come across a thirty-second clip of someone speaking who was cut out from a larger speech. The user may have either made a false claim about the clip or used hashtags to make a misleading implication. This is called taking things out of context. The program I like to use to judge the authenticity of videos is called InVID, a simple program you can download to your laptop that lets you do a reverse video search. The other tactic I would use is to search the title of the clip online to find the original clip and possibly a transcript you can place side by side for readability measures.

PubMed Search: Home remedies are a classic on social media. I've come across people claiming grapes and cannabis can cure cancer. So where's the first place I go when these things pop up? PubMed, the repository of scientific research studies. Keywords to use to solidify and distinguish your search would be preclinical studies, which occur in animals and through test tubes, and clinical studies, which involve humans. If only preclinical studies are available, then whether something will be an effective treatment on humans hasn't been tested. Other databases, such as the National Center for Biotechnology Information, also have research studies.

Government, agency, and company websites: While this may seem like a cliché tactic, a lot of information is often overlooked on social media because no one takes the time to visit official websites. For instance, I came across posts Apple was creating a smart ring. However, no press releases on Apple's website confirmed this. Doing a simple search can save you a lot of time and a lot of trouble.

I've also been developing two models I believe can help someone fight misinformation in the *long-term*: the curiosity paradigm and the check-your-bias chart. Cultivating skills needed to fight misinformation can only be done when a person puts both models to use. I like to call this a "multi-structured approach." Let's explore both models:

THE CURIOSITY PARADIGM

Throughout my journalism career, I have put my power of skepticism to good use. I would constantly question everything around me, raise important discussions about issues that weren't being solved, or explore areas that weren't being ventured enough. But curiosity is really what drove and fostered my skepticism. To me, curiosity and skepticism aren't the same. They build *off each other*.

Skepticism is an "attitude of doubt or a disposition to incredulity either in general or toward a particular object," according to Merriam-Webster. A lot of critical thinking, reasoning, and analysis is done in this stage. When you scrutinize whether an infographic in a social media post shows accurate figures or whether the source behind the image is credible, you are using the power of skepticism.

Curiosity, on the other hand, is an "inquisitive interest in other's concerns," according to Merriam-Webster. You ask questions, search for truth, and try to gather as much knowledge about a subject matter as you can, which leads you to become skeptical. You become gradually aware of what is right and what appears to look wrong. But to reach this stage of skepticism, you first *have* to build your curiosity.

That's why I developed a paradigm people can use to determine whether they are applying their urge of curiosity—a strong desire to know something—with five basic techniques related to combating misinformation:

1. asking questions,

2. determining source-based credibility,

3. having a good source list,

4. applying research skills, and

5. changing mindset.

A paradigm isn't necessarily a scale you measure yourself on. A paradigm is a "generalized model that provides a viewpoint from which the real world may be investigated," according to Oxford Reference. So essentially, my paradigm is trying to create a viewpoint or perspective in which curiosity, when applied in a deliberate manner, can strengthen basic fact-checking techniques.

1. Asking Questions

First, individuals must be willing to ask questions *consistently,* a strategy of news reporting. Asking questions is not only the heart of journalism, but also a way to ensure every piece of information is being challenged without turning a blind eye.

Questions don't necessarily need to be open ended or complex; sometimes, they can be as simple as "Where did this statistic come from?" or "How many people engaged in this activity?" The smallest questions can have the most impact.

So isn't a person who is asking questions already being curious? Not necessarily.

The difference between a person deliberately being curious and mindlessly inquiring is in how they structure the questions. The way this can be measured is through relevance, impact, and context. Relevance refers to how specific you are in asking questions that can get you answers, impact is whether you ask questions that are complex and answer all dimensions of an issue, and context is understanding the background behind an issue.

Let's say you are investigating whether cancer rates have increased since the vaccine rollout was introduced. Asking someone whether COVID-19 rates has increased is not going to answer your question, since you want to focus on cancer *incidence* rates, or the number of times someone has gotten diagnosed with cancer in a given period of time, which is relevant.

At the same time, if you are asking an expert whether the COVID-19 vaccines cause cancer, questions revolving around how mRNA vaccines work is good context and whether any clinical trials or research studies show this claim is impactful.

2. Determining Source-Based Credibility

Next is determining source-based credibility. Credibility is unique in it tends to be in the eye of the beholder; in other words, people think those who are like them are the most credible. So even though it is a receiver-based construct, credibility should really be measured based on a combination of the following:

- Expert authority:
    - Do they have degrees? Have they done research studies? Are they the right person to speak about the topic? Have they spoken about this topic before?

- Influence:
    - Are they verified? Do they have profile pages that list where they went to school? Do they have a LinkedIn profile?

- Compassion:
    - Do they seem to care about others? Have they spoken about the dangers of misinformation before?
- Competence:
    - Have any of their research studies been successful? Have they spoken to journalists or fact-checkers about the topic?
- Trustworthiness:
    - Have they spread accurate information before, or have they spread misinformation?

A truly curious person would make sure to check out these avenues before concluding someone is right or even determining whether the authority behind a social media post is credible.

3. Having a Good Source List

This goes along with the third technique, which is having a good source list. In other words, a person has to take the extra time to flesh out who they follow on Instagram and Facebook because that's what would allow them to see whether they are getting *consistent accurate* information.

Here's where curiosity would come into play: using the components of source-based credibility I have listed above to flesh out that list.

4. Applying Research Skills

That requires doing *research,* the fourth component of the paradigm. For instance, I could be following the Children's Health Defense, and I might think it is a committed organization helping children with health problems. But that's wrong. Any person who does their research knows the organization, created by antivaxxer Robert F. Kennedy Jr., is dedicated to spreading COVID-19 antivaccine content, according to the Center for Countering Digital Hate 2021 Disinformation Dozen report.

5. Changing Mindset

The last basic technique for combating misinformation is changing your mindset. What this means is a person questions their biases and where they may be coming from: Is it their family or their friends? Is it a certain group of people? Is it something they've read online? How are their political views being shaped? Is it because of a certain candidate's platform? Being curious about oneself can help you break out of a "filter bubble," or a bubble of ideas and beliefs that shape a person's worldview.

THE CHECK-YOUR-BIAS CHART

The other model I created was the check-your-bias chart. This chart is fairly simple:

Check-Your-Bias Chart

Social media post aligns with your beliefs.	Social media post doesn't align with your beliefs.
Initial reaction: You think the content is accurate without doing research.	Initial reaction: You don't think the content is accurate, and you haven't done any research.
First take: You know the content is accurate after doing your research.	First take: You know the content is not accurate after doing your research
Second take: You know the content is not accurate after doing your research.	Second take: You know the content is accurate after doing your research.

There are basically three ways this can go on either side of the spectrum. You come across a social media post that aligns with your beliefs. At first, you think the content is accurate because of factors related to confirmation bias. You can either maintain that initial reaction or *do your research*. After you do research, you either determine whether the content is actually accurate, thereby marking you right, or showing whether it was wrong.

The same goes vice versa. I came across a social media post from a politician from an opposing political party and my initial reaction was the content they posted was false. I could either keep my initial reaction or do my research. So I did my research and I figured out I was right. But I could also do the research and figure out the content is right.

The way someone deals with the second take, which can lead to cognitive dissonance in which someone is at crossroads with the research they've come across not aligning with their already established beliefs, is through a change in mindset. If you are willing to accept the content is either false or right, and you were wrong after doing your research, I believe you've successfully checked your bias in the situation.

These are just a few methods that are effective in fighting misinformation, both in the short-term and the long-terms. You can add on to these techniques as you continue your journey and share these tips with others too. Throughout this book, you've learned all sorts of new concepts and tricks, and my hope for you is you can take some of the knowledge I imparted in this chapter and the information given by experts to change your life in a positive way.

ACKNOWLEDGMENTS

This book would not have been possible without the support of such a wonderful community. First and foremost, I want to thank my parents for supporting me throughout this endeavor and for supporting my dream of becoming a journalist. I don't think I could have gotten this far without them. I want to give a special shoutout to my mom for helping me design the cover page of my book, which turned out spectacular.

I also want to thank my sister for always being there for me, for teaching me about the healthcare field, and for supporting my dreams. You learn a lot from having a sibling, and this journey would not have been successful without her.

Thank you so much to Marina Pitofsky, who helped edit my book, provided feedback on chapters, and encouraged me throughout the journey. When I first met Marina, I knew she would always be there for me, and she always has been! From my internship at *USA Today* to this book writing journey I took, she was always supportive of all the work I published and have written. I would not have gotten this far along in my journey without her.

To my wonderful author community, thank you for being a part of my inner circle, cheering me on, and taking the time to read my chapters. Thank you to Suha Hafeez,

Sofia Syed, Eric Koester, Lamar Love, Timothy Gibson, Noland McCaskill, Jon Poletti, Jayavishnu Nattanmai, Shiva Dhanuskodi, Cecilia Aguilar, Sidonia Cannon, Nicolas Macotto, Poojitha Tanjore, Priscilla Yun, Anna Bertino, Gabrielle Buffaloe, Kat Camberg, Samantha Gibbs, Bob Butler, Maanasa Valluri, Ravi Rajaram, Udaya Allu, Venkataganesh Thoppae, Amritha Premnath, Sanjib Rajbhandari, Brendan Gordon, Alison O'Leary, Anil Verma, Marc Saulino, Emerson Davis, Lane Schwager, Sathvika Madisetty, Emily Gilmore, Nancy Mantelli, Rashmika Premnath, Jennifer Karchmer, Batoul Hasan, Raymond Ruiz, Alexandra Bowman, Sundaresh Oblan, Daniel Funke, Alex Begley, Mahesh Kumar, Emily Simons, Aditya Shahi, Ankitha Iyer, Jayla Brown, Thai Nguyen, Manasi Mudumbai, Asha Aravindakshan, Denise Durgin, Terri Nakamura, and Chandu Gogineni.

To all the journalists, fact-checkers, psychologists, researchers, and countless other experts I consulted while writing the book, thank you. I wanted to give a shoutout to Jon Roozenbeek, Emily Vraga, Shannon Poulsen, Thomas Hill, Chirag Shah, Filippo Menczer, Shane Creevy, Adrian Hon, Reed Berkowitz, Mick West, Steven Sloman, Jolanda Jetten, Anke Richter, Lenka Perron, Steve Eichel, Greg Toppo, Bill Adair, Harrison Mantas, David Rapp, Emmanuel C. Ohuabunwa, Diane Benscoter, Michelle Mello, Matthew Baum, Daniel Funke, Dan Romer, Steven Herman, Tonya Mosley, Robert Hernandez, Jennifer Karchmer, Chloe Jones, Collette Watson, Karen Jubanyik, and Ernest Owens. I also wanted to thank Morgan Givens, P. Kim Bui, Alice Bell, Ariana Freeman, and Lu Xiao for taking the time to meet with me during the book-writing process.

My mentor, Kiah Haslett, has been there for me every step of the way, whether it be in writing this book or cheering me on in my internships. My calls with her were the highlight of each week, and she would always ask me how I was doing and how my book was coming along. She is the best.

Finally, to all my future readers out there, thank you for picking up this book and being a part of my journey.

APPENDIX

CHAPTER ONE:

Allcott, Hunt and Matthew Gentzkow. "Social Media and Fake News in the 2016 Election." *Journal of Economic Perspectives* 31, no. 2 (Spring 2017): 211–236. https://pubs.aeaweb.org/doi/pdfplus/10.1257/jep.31.2.211?source=post_page

Baxter, Michael. "Military Arrests SCJ Sonia Sotomayor." Real Raw News, February 18, 2022. Accessed March 3, 2022. https://realrawnews.com/2022/02/military-arrests-scj-sonia-sotomayor/

Center for Countering Digital Hate. "The Disinformation Dozen." Accessed February 27, 2022. https://www.counterhate.com/_files/ugd/f4d9b9_b7cedc0553604720b7137f8663366ee5.pdf

Centers for Disease Control and Prevention. "COVID-19 Vaccines for People Who Would Like to Have a Baby." Accessed February 27, 2022, https://www.cdc.gov/coronavirus/2019-ncov/vaccines/planning-for-pregnancy.html

Centers for Disease Control and Prevention. "Misconceptions about Seasonal Flu and Flu Vaccines." Accessed February 27, 2022, https://www.cdc.gov/flu/prevent/misconceptions.htm

Funke, Daniel. "Weeks After His Death, Most of Paul Horner's Fake News Sites are Down. So What's Left?" Poynter Institute. Accessed February 27, 2022. https://www.poynter.org/fact-checking/2017/weeks-after-his-death-most-of-paul-horner%C2%92s-fake-news-sites-are-down-so-what%C2%92s-left/

Graphika. "Secondary Infektion at a Glance." Accessed February 27, 2022. https://secondaryinfektion.org/report/secondary-infektion-at-a-glance/

Kochi, Sudiksha. "No, Meghan Markle didn't tweet about Oprah Winfrey. Tweet is from a Fake Account." *PolitiFact,* March 17, 2021. https://www.politifact.com/factchecks/2021/mar/17/viral-image/no-meghan-markle-didnt-tweet-about-oprah-winfrey-t/

Merriam Webster. s.v. "fabricated (v.)." Accessed February 27, 2022. https://www.merriam-webster.com/dictionary/fabricate

PolitiFact. "PolitiFact: The Origin Story." *Politifact.* May 11, 2021. YouTube video, 4:53. https://www.youtube.com/watch?v=eA7VNQY9B4c

Vraga, Emily and Leticia Bode. "Correction Experiences on Social Media During COVID-19." *Sage Journals* 7, no. 2 (April 2021). https://doi.org/10.1177/20563051211008829

Wallace, Caroline. "Obama Did Not Ban the Pledge." FactCheck.org, September 2, 2016. Accessed February 27, 2022. https://www.factcheck.org/2016/09/obama-did-not-ban-the-pledge/

CHAPTER TWO:

Britt, Michael. "The Elaboration Likelihood Model Explained." May 15, 2013. YouTube video, 1:50. https://www.youtube.com/watch?v=VlqUPJ_LCrs

Edison Research. "The Top 50 Most Listened to Podcasts in the U.S. q2 2021." August 9, 2021. Accessed February 27, 2022. https://www.edisonresearch.com/the-top-50-most-listened-to-podcasts-in-the-u-s-q2-2021/

Garrett, R. Kelly, Robert Bond, and Shannon Poulsen. "Too Many People Think Satirical News is Real." Ohio State News, August 16, 2019. Accessed March 2, 2022. https://news.osu.edu/too-many-people-think-satirical-news-is-real/

Hameleers, Michael, Thomas E. Powell, Toni G.L.A. Van Der Meer & Lieke Bos. "A Picture Paints a Thousand Lies? The Effects and Mechanisms of Multimodal Disinformation and Rebuttals Disseminated via Social Media," Political Communication, 37:2, 281-301, DOI: 10.1080/10584609.2019.1674979

Hays, Tom and Larry Neumeister. "Ghislaine Maxwell convicted in Epstein sex abuse case." Associated Press. December 29, 2021. Accessed March 4, 2022. https://apnews.com/article/ghislaine-maxwell-convicted-jeffrey-epstein-trial-verdict-63a71a2825eab41184a79e37bb967e90

Kochi, Sudiksha. "Fact Check: Altered Photo Falsely Claims to Show Elon Musk with a Robot He Built as a Child." USA Today, November 10, 2021. Accessed March 2, 2022. https://www.usatoday.com/story/news/factcheck/2021/11/10/fact-check-altered-photo-claims-show-young-elon-musk-robot/6336248001/

Kochi, Sudiksha. "Fact Check: CNN Graphic Related to Ghislaine Maxwell Trial and Jeffrey Epstein has been Altered." USA Today, December 21, 2021. Accessed March 2, 2022. https://www.usatoday.com/story/news/factcheck/2021/12/21/fact-check-cnn-graphic-related-maxwell-trial-has-been-altered/8925000002/

Kochi, Sudiksha. "Fact Check: False Claim That Pumpkin Seeds Can Treat Worms and Parasites in the Body." USA Today, December 17, 2021. Accessed March 2, 2022. https://www.usatoday.com/story/news/factcheck/2021/12/17/fact-check-pumpkin-seeds-not-effective-against-worms-and-parasites/6508822001/

Kochi, Sudiksha. "Fact Check: False Claim That 'Shark Tank' Judges Endorsed a Keto Diet Pill." USA Today, October 11, 2021. Accessed March 2, 2022. https://www.usatoday.com/story/news/factcheck/2021/10/11/fact-check-false-claim-shark-tank-judges-endorsed-keto-diet-pill/6035141001/

Madhani, Aamer. "Biden vows US to act decisively if Russia invades Ukraine." *The Associated Press*, January 2, 2022. Accessed March 2, 2022. https://apnews.com/article/joe-biden-europe-russia-ukraine-united-states-ab28bf759bf22853c24860498dc651c1

Minhaj, Hasan. *Patriot Act with Hasan Minhaj,* directed by Hasan Minhaj. (2018). Netflix. https://www.imdb.com/title/tt8080054/

National Institute of Diabetes and Digestive and Kidney Diseases. "Prescription Medications to Treat Overweight & Obesity." Accessed February 27, 2022. https://www.niddk.nih.gov/health-information/weight-management/prescription-medications-treat-overweight-obesity

O'Rourke, Ciara. "No, This Isn't a Real AOC Quote About Truckers." *PolitiFact,* Febuary 7, 2022. Accessed March 2, 2022. https://www.politifact.com/factchecks/2022/feb/07/viral-image/no-isnt-real-aoc-quote-about-truckers/

O'Rourke, Ciara. "Video shows child shouting an expletive at Jill Biden." PolitiFact, December 1, 2021. Accessed March 2, 2022. https://www.politifact.com/factchecks/2021/dec/01/viral-image/video-child-shouting-expletive-jill-biden-has-been/

Sang-Hun, Choe. "Kim Jong-un's Absence and North Korea's Silence Keep Rumor Mill Churning." The New York Times, April 26, 2020. Accessed February 27, 2022. https://www.nytimes.com/2020/04/26/world/asia/kim-jong-un-absence-north-korea.html

The Onion. "Biden Vows That If Russia Invades Ukraine, U.S. Will Invade One Country of Equivalent Value." Accessed March 2, 2022. https://www.theonion.com/biden-vows-that-if-russia-invades-ukraine-u-s-will-in-1848401421

The Onion. "Cancer Researcher Develops Feelings for Lab Rat While Working Long Nights Alone Together." Accessed March 2, 2022. https://www.theonion.com/cancer-researcher-develops-feelings-for-lab-rat-while-w-1848558646

Wardle, Claire. "Fake news. It's complicated." *Medium,* February 16, 2017. https://medium.com/1st-draft/fake-news-its-complicated-d0f773766c79

Young, Dannagal G., Kathleen Hall Jamieson, Shannon Poulsen, and Abigail Goldring. "Fact-Checking Effectiveness as a Function of Format and Tone: Evaluating FactCheck.org and FlackCheck.org." Journalism & Mass Communication Quarterly 95, no. 1

(July 6, 2017). 49-75. Accessed March 3, 2022. https://doi.org/10.1177%2F1077699017710453

CHAPTER THREE:

Kochi, Sudiksha. "Fact check: Viral video shows 2015 explosion in China, not in Ukraine." USA Today, February 24, 2022. Accessed March 2, 2022. https://www.usatoday.com/story/news/factcheck/2022/02/24/fact-check-video-shows-2015-explosion-china-not-ukraine/6922882001/

CHAPTER FOUR:

Harvard University. "Chemtrails Conspiracy Theory." Accessed March 2, 2022. https://keith.seas.harvard.edu/chemtrails-conspiracy-theory

Hon, Adrian. "What ARGs Can Teach Us About QAnon." MSSV, August 2, 2020. Accessed March 2, 2022. https://mssv.net/2020/08/02/what-args-can-teach-us-about-qanon/

Kinzen. Accessed March 2, 2022. https://www.kinzen.com/company

Merriam Webster. s.v. "Apophenia (n.)." Accessed March 4, 2022. https://www.merriam-webster.com/dictionary/apophenia

Metabunk (forum). "Utah Drone video of UFO [Probably an Insect Zip-By]." January 13, 2019. Accessed March 2, 2022. https://www.metabunk.org/threads/utah-drone-video-of-ufo-probably-an-insect-zip-by.10370/

CHAPTER FIVE:

Corporate Finance Institute. "What is Maslow's Hierarchy of Needs?" Accessed March 4, 2022. https://corporatefinanceinstitute.com/resources/knowledge/other/maslows-hierarchy-of-needs/

Mathieu, Cynthia. "Social desirability bias." Accessed March 4, 2022. http://www.sciencedirect.com/topics/psychology/social-desirability

McKay, Adam, dir. *Don't Look Up*. 2021: Netflix. https://www.imdb.com/title/tt11286314/

PolitiFact. "Mind Control and Fact-Checking with Dr. Steven Hassan." June 1, 2020. YouTube video. https://www.youtube.com/watch?v=60ExKs80ygo

Rapp, David and Nikita Salovich. "Can't We Just Disregard Fake News? The Consequences of Exposure to Inaccurate Information." Sage Journals 5, no. 2 (September 6, 2018) 232-239. https://doi.org/10.1177/2372732218785193

Romer, Dan and Kathleen Jamieson. "Conspiratorial Thinking, Selective Exposure to Conservative Media, and Response to COVID-19 in the US." Social Science & Medicine 291 (December 2021). https://doi.org/10.1016/j.socscimed.2021.114480

Tavernise, Sabrina. "Trump Just Used Us and Our Fear: One Woman's Journey Out of QAnon." The New York Times. January 29, 2021. Accessed March 4, 2022. https://www.nytimes.com/2021/01/29/us/leaving-qanon-conspiracy.html

CHAPTER SIX:

De Smedt, Tom, and Verica Rupar. "Spreading conspiracy theories on Twitter." Media Diversity Institute, December 2020. Accessed March 2, 2022. https://static1.squarespace.com/static/5ee500d316a2470c370596d3/t/5fe3207446bf310e1611a53b/1608720522110/QAnon+Report+2.pdf

Karakoulaki, Marianna. "Antisemitic Narratives Find Ground in COVID-19 Anti-Vax Conspiracy Theories." Covinform.

Accessed March 2, 2022. https://www.covinform.eu/2021/12/20/antisemitic-narratives-in-covid-19-anti-vax-conspiracy-theories/

Kochi, Sudiksha. "Fact Check: Image Claiming to Show Barack Obama's Birth Certificate is Fake." USA Today, October 13, 2021. Accessed March 2, 2022. https://www.usatoday.com/story/news/factcheck/2021/10/13/fact-check-obama-born-hawaii-not-kenya/5898722001/

Kochi, Sudiksha. "How Does the QAnon Conspiracy Theory Spread Online?" *Media Diversity Institute,* February 2, 2021. https://www.media-diversity.org/how-does-qanon-spread-online/

Media Diversity Institute. "QAnon and the Growing Conspiracy Theory Trend on Social Media." June 2020. Accessed March 2, 2022. https://static1.squarespace.com/static/5ee500d316a2470c370596d3/t/5f1813b4c9031f13d52ad25f/1595413465022/QAnon+Report.pdf

Richter, Anke. "Conspiracy Cults and the Mental Health Pandemic." September 19, 2020. Accessed March 4, 2022. https://thespinoff.co.nz/society/19-09-2020/conspiracy-cults-and-the-mental-health-pandemic

Richter, Anke. "How Alternative Festivals Became Platforms for Conspiracy Theorists." The Spinoff. April 21, 2021. Accessed March 4, 2022. https://thespinoff.co.nz/society/21-04-2021/how-alternative-festivals-became-platforms-for-conspiracy-theorists

Tavernise, Sabrina. "Trump Just Used Us and Our Fear: One Woman's Journey out of QAnon." The New York Times. Jan. 29, 2021. Accessed March 2, 2022. https://www.nytimes.com/2021/01/29/us/leaving-qanon-conspiracy.html

CHAPTER SEVEN:

Gichuhi, Grace. "No, video of huge moon viewed from somewhere 'between Russia and Canada' not real." Africa Check, June 25, 2021. Accessed March 2, 2022. https://africacheck.org/fact-checks/fbchecks/no-video-huge-moon-viewed-somewhere-between-russia-and-canada-not-real

Kochi, Sudiksha. "Fact Check: False Claim That Celebrities' Deaths Linked to Child Sex Trafficking Documentary." USA Today, January 18, 2022. Accessed March 2, 2022. https://www.usatoday.com/story/news/factcheck/2022/01/18/fact-check-no-link-between-celebrities-deaths-documentary-project/9169646002/

Ng, John. "The Four Faces of Face." Mediate, May 2008. Accessed March 2, 2022. https://www.mediate.com/articles/the_four_faces_of_face.cfm#bio

Rosenfeld, Michael, Thomas Reuben, and Sonia Hausen. "Disintermediating Your Friends: How Online Dating in the United States Displaces Other Ways of Meeting." Proceedings of the National Academy of Sciences 116, no. 36 (August 20, 2019). https://doi.org/10.1073/pnas.1908630116

CHAPTER EIGHT:

Botsman, Rachel. "We've stopped trusting institutions and started trusting strangers." Filmed June 2016 at TEDSummit, Banff, Canada. TED video, 16:59. https://www.ted.com/talks/rachel_botsman_we_ve_stopped_trusting_institutions_and_started_trusting_strangers

CHAPTER NINE:

Center for Countering Digital Hate. "Disinformation Dozen." Accessed March 4, 2022. https://www.counterhate.com/disinformationdozen

Merriam Webster. s.v. "Skepticism (n.)." Accessed March 4, 2022. https://www.merriam-webster.com/dictionary/skepticism

Merriam Webster. s.v. "Curiosity (n.)." Accessed March 4, 2022. https://www.merriam-webster.com/dictionary/curiosity

Oxford Reference. s.v. "Paradigm." https://www.oxfordreference.com/view/10.1093/oi/authority.20110803100305726#:~:text=Quick%20Reference,derived%20from%20the%20real%20world

Scanlan, Chip. "If Your Mother Says She Loves You: A Reporter's Cautionary Tale." *Poynter Institute,* April 17, 2003. Accessed March 3, 2022. https://www.poynter.org/reporting-editing/2003/if-your-mother-says-she-loves-you-a-reporters-cautionary-tale/

Social Security Administration. "Number of Social Security recipients from 2018 to 2021." Accessed March 4, 2022. https://www.ssa.gov/OACT/ProgData/icp.html